WINTER SKY

Winter Sky

NEW AND SELECTED POEMS, 1968–2008

COLEMAN BARKS

The University of Georgia Press | Athens & London

logo

Publication of this book was supported in part by the
Kenneth Coleman Series in Georgia History and Culture.

Published by the University of Georgia Press
Athens, Georgia 30602
www.ugapress.org
© 2008 by Coleman Barks
All rights reserved
Designed by
Set in Minion and Legacy by Graphic Composition, Inc.
Printed and bound by
The paper in this book meets the guidelines for
permanence and durability of the Committee on
Production Guidelines for Book Longevity of the
Council on Library Resources.

Printed in the United States of America
12 11 10 09 08 C 5 4 3 2 1

Library of Congress Cataloging-in-Publication Data

British Library Cataloging-in-Publication Data available

for this funny family

CONTENTS

1967–1977

FROM *WE'RE LAUGHING AT THE DAMAGE* (1977)

FROM *NEW WORDS* (1976)

FROM *THE JUICE* (1972)

ACKNOWLEDGMENTS

Some of the new poems here appeared first in the following periodicals: *Five Points, Café Review* and *The Secret of Salt: An Indigenous Journal.* The other poems are from the following books: *The Juice* (New York: Harper and Row, 1972); *New Words* (Austell, Ga.: Burnt Hickory Press, 1976); *We're Laughing at the Damage* (Davidson, N.C.: Briarpatch Press, 1977); *Club: Granddaughter Poems* (Athens, Ga.: Maypop Books, 2001); *Scrapwood Man* (Athens, Ga.: Maypop Books, 2007).

In the late 1970s I had a dream of being a bookstore. On the lefthand counter is a huge open book with raised gold type. It is in all languages—German, Arabic, Cherokee, Chinese—and mixed in with the different alphabets are musical signatures, algebraic signs, figures from physics. It is very beautiful. It is everything. It costs $700 and I happen to have that much on me. I feel a deep longing for it, but something rational comes over me. I reason that I will never learn all those languages, so I will never be able to *read* the book if I buy it. I turn away from that counter and from the miraculous book. In the center of the bookstore is a small performance area, with a lifesize wooden statue of Jesus. A monk in a dark hood is standing face to face with Jesus, pouring lighter fluid over his head and lighting it. As it flares up, he mumbles unintelligibly into the burning face. It is a ceremony called *Embarrassing the Christ*. I turn to the counter on my right where there is a stack of round emblems. I look through them. A girl, pointing over my shoulder, says *That one is yours*. It has a whisk broom at the top, a tiny down-feather in the center, and a yin-yang line down the center that becomes a road and then a shallow stream with two black dogs at the bottom, padding along, companionable in the splashing, hanging out, exploring things together. I aspire to the gait and taoist nonchalance of those two dogs. I certainly *overthought* the decision *not* to buy the golden book, but am glad the dream did not end with me walking out of the store *owning* that astounding tome. The dream feels like a life-dream, and it would not be *my* life if it had ended that way. Each of those scenes is probably an emblem for a stage in my life. I do adore *whatever it is* in consciousness (or outside of it) that gives us such dreams, and also what receives and remembers them, what writes them down devotedly. Then whatever it is that phrases them as splices for the wiring of a poem to keep the current moving. I love all that. But it is with the mystery that *gives* dreams that I would have more conversation.

I have always loved emblems. I had a strange collection of advertising logos as a child. I would cut them out of magazines and paste them in ledgers. Maybe this poetry collection is a continuation of that. There's an emblem of how an aluminum canoe floats on stream water with no one in it, One showing how light is inside a fire and coming out of it too, onto our sleeping faces. One about how it feels to be a snake gliding out of its skin on an early summer day. Socrates lecturing from inside a hanging basket-cage. That last is not here. That is the wonderful emblem of what *thinking* looks like, from Aristophanes' *The Clouds*. Socrates calls the basket his *thinkery*. Socrates walking free is what we're after.

Rumi suggests that we listen for presences inside poems. Say we are a lineage, a complicated layered presence, composed of all we have loved and all who have loved us. My beloved cousin, Tom Lamar. Dostoyevsky, Lao Tze. My crowd mixes with your crowd. Language, poetry especially, helps that converging of currents. I am continually amazed with the process. And now that Rumi has entered the room, you could say that he and Shams are luring us toward obliteration, into ever widening, deepening, skies of loving. Shams once said of Rumi that the writing came through him in three kinds of scripts:

One that he could read and only he.
One that he and others could read.
And one that neither he nor anyone else
could read. I am that *third script*.

The presence of Shams Tabriz is the great mystery living inside Rumi's poetry. The cave lion. Every poetry collection should have such a wild center, such a soul. We wait for some more alive presence to enter us, something that will come in and begin the friendship and the work that will feel like cosmic play. Often the voice speaking a Wallace Stevens poem seems to be expecting such a visitation. (See "Chocorua to its Neighbor.") That is what I love about those long, astonishing Stevens poems. You feel an unsayable presence impinging, approaching. Like a shadow moving across a mountain, *rugged roy. . . .* Ulysses returning to Penelope ("The World as Meditation") as a *form of fire* lifting itself above the horizon. It is the longing for an incandescent friendship. You feel it in Whitman's beach-wending poems too.

The first poetry reading I ever gave was at the Presbyterian Student Center in Athens, Georgia. October 1967. The assistant minister came up afterward. Everything doesn't *have* to be about sex, she scolded. I forget my reply. But the source of much of my poesis then, the energy propelling it, was Whitman's *Blind loving wrestling touch, sheath'd hooded sharp-tooth'd touch.* Words were a way to caress experience, to hold and taste it. My writing has obviously grown out of my life. In forty years of making poems there have been three waves of creativity, overlapping but more or less distinct, the strongest being the one that rose in the late 1970s and played out around 2002, producing three books: *Gourd Seed, Tentmaking,* and *Club.* The first wave began in the mid-1960s and lasted into the late 70s. Three books came from that too, *The Juice, New Words* and *We're Laughing at the Damage.* The third is still building. It is the most interesting to me, so I put it first. *Scrapwood Man* is the only book from that so far. So the rough arrangement of this book is those three waves of making in reverse chronological order. The earliest deals with the matter of three boundary times, having children (Choosing, "begat begat"), the death of my parents (the "New Words" sequence), and divorce (the "Laughing at the Damage" sequence). The poems, whatever else they may be about, cluster around those events, the joys and griefs of them, and they are solidly grounded in the body, as the sweet assistant Presbyterian observed.

The second section treats other boundaries. When children go off to college ("New Year's Day Nap"), the death of friends ("Small Talk," "Elegy for John Seawright"), changes in the nature and intensity of desire ("In the Woods, You and I," "Wagtail," "Two-Hour Wait in Toronto," "Bedclothes," "A Walk in the Botanical Garden"), having grandchildren (the Club poems). There are also poems about the fear of infidelity ("Question," "Kindling"), my fear of alcohol addiction ("Some Orange Juice," "Hymenoptera," "Lard Gourd"), and there are poems that take the dare of making public antiwar statements ("Becoming Milton," "Just This Once"). There are poems too that celebrate the privacy of a retreat from public exposure ("Book Tour Cure for Talking Too Much in Public," "A Wish," "Fightingtown Creek," "An Up-Till-Now-Uncelebrated Joy").

The third section remembers getting over a speech defect in adolescence ("Car Trips," "The Return of Professor Dumwhistle") and anticipates the approach to the painful late boundary of losing one's bearings ("Losing It"), as well as my own upcoming death ("The Center"). This last theme has been present in earlier sections too ("No Finale," "Driving Back from the Mountains"), as has that grandest desolation boundary in a lifetime, the death, even if just for a moment, of the ego ("Nickajack Cave," "Choosing," "Kingsnake," "New Year's Day Nap," "Night Creek," "Silo," "Spring Violets," "The Tree," "The Premise," "Reading in Bed"). Images from dreams, and people met there, have been crucial for me in various rites of recognition, initiation, and valediction. The themes are everybody's themes. But this is no way to talk about one's own poems. Compartmentalizing does disservice, and it's a lie, the linear scheme. Poem-making for me is more a vatic, ecstatic meander. Documenting the seven, or seventeen, ages of man is not the point. Those boundaries are bases on which imagination builds, doing whatever it is it does, something akin to dreaming. The mysterious motions of soul, those thrive somehow through making poems. Verve, intricacy, stamina, honesty, foolishness, illumination, determination—various qualities begin to flourish. If there is an underlying subject, let it be that engendering of *qualities*.

NEW POEMS

This is meant to praise
the single thing living in the middle
that follows no rules we yet know,
or maybe ever will,
though it may be weighed
like any sack of pecans, its mass estimated
at three hundred million times that of the sun.

Praise to what we must give in to,
the big laziness, spiracle blowhole,
where matter comes breathing out,
where matter gets sucked back in
to be nothing, or changed to a lightshaft
a trillion trillion lightyears tall
pouring periodically from this whirlpool
that has no bottom. Does some rhythm
coming round ordain this making/unmaking?

In praise of the tao that is sometimes milk,
that accepts us into it as identical
beveled alabaster lozenges, what
we become in the moment of dying.

Praise to our knowing *so little*
of the waterwheels turning
inside our cells so tiny,
and the churning barrel so vast.

Beside which we are plywood cutouts,
caricatures of emotional states
we have participated in.

These are set up, propped about
the milksource maelstrom, plastered
with mud. So we are caught

in mid-gesture, humiliated, ecstatic,
disappointed in love, being honored
by the assembly, theatre lobby displays.

This is in praise of how we are gone
into that which dissolves us,
not stuck in reward or punishment,
but refined clean
into soap-slick rectangules.

In praise of the riddle
that feeds us the next intuition.

In praise of the wilderness
that has a teacher at its core,
of our being lost in that.

A great sky-mackerel swims across,
as a long cormorant dive
inkbrush stroke curves against it.

Praise to the friend I meet in dream.
His strong arm points me deeper
into a cave, where saints and wildmen
sit meditating on ledges
like candle sconces irregularly placed
on the wall of a towering cylinder-shaft.

In praise of the place he finds
for me on the left side
of a wooden chair.

Praise to this most constant love
I have known, the never-written
solitude with no meaning.

. . .

The Milky Way was named in prehistory,
before it was known to be our unique
community seen from the side.

That which gives our galactic whiparms
their long elliptical motion
has yet no name. Chatoyant catseye,
fully awake in the spatial dark, *Bijou,*
beautiful eater of beauty, however it is
we love our lives is how we love you.

Astronomy or molecular microscopy
cannot quite be felt as living experience,
can they? Still a tidal balance of inner
and outer quivers, confused.
Praise the tremble.

The day I was born, April 23, 1937,
the *New York Times* had a front page picture
of what tin looks like through
the just-invented electron microscope.
Waves of silvery surf.

Such enormous amounts we do not know,
like if there is another world,
and how the unfoldings go on beyond this.

Praise the unlimited ignorance.

I am petting an owl *in flight.*
My hand strokes the grey-black-tan
featherlayered design on its back
as it flies in the night.

Death-bird talks to me, says,
Soon you must give up your DNA.

It is a huge extravagance
hiring a car to get home
the final sixty-seven miles,
having missed the last shuttle
from the Atlanta airport to Athens
by five minutes. So I enjoy it,
napping or nearly napping
on the middle van seat.

It is a raining February night.
A cheerful Ethiopian man is driving,
steady and very fast, passing the trucks
with their vast sleeping compartments
behind their cabs, spaceships.

It feels like I have not watched
traffic sideways since I was a child.
At seventy, going eighty, eighty-five.

The drips on the sidewindows
do their slow slide toward the rear.
How can that be? What is the physics
of such slowness?

We are going fast, but the drips
are finding a leisurely way,
stopping awhile, shivering, continuing on,
as though making watery decisions,
this magnificently dawdling troop
of Taoist masters, who arrive at
the rubber edging of my window
from up in the nowhere of this night's coldfront.

· · ·

I graph with fingers
their progress on the convex pane.

Whatever presences we are blessed by,
we must bless others with,
to keep the blessings moving along,
the nearly formless ones
who drop vertically in,
and just for a sideways drawn-out
moment are with us, and we see them
held supinely in the custody
of an amicable Ethiopian man.

We feel them sliding through
and out the bottom of being
as they become songs and sentences,
the notions and beauty of the liquid
fire of presence, in people we meet,
in the nightair we breathe cupfuls of.

I never saw light like that in everyone's eyes
the misty-rain morning we dug a hole
and buried Bawa Muhaiyaddeen.

He always called us the *lightpoints*,
the jewel-lights of his eyes. We traded
pointed spades back and forth digging
in the rocky Pennsylvania earth, placed him
curled in the bottom without a box,
on his side with a handful of ground
in his hand next to his cheek,
then filled in, around and over.

When the grave was up to within two feet
of ground level, I was in the hole by myself
packing the dirt with my boots, not noticing
that others were waiting with more fill
to shovel in. A voice says quietly,
Do you want to go with him? Just lie down.

It was like mirrorglow, or water ripples
on a cliff, the light in everyone's eyes
that December morning.

I have tried to write
in praise of the dew
and what it does,
condensing nightair
into invisible eyedroppers
of cold water that wash
the hands of the grassblades.

It is that
sudden wet breakage
that we love.

In Union Springs, Alabama, at the Dollar General.
White lady doing the register
says to the black man customer in front of me,
Fish gone fishin.
Black guy says, I caught a five-pound bream.

I say, a five-pound bream?
One pound. If I caught a five-pound bream,
I wouldn't be here. I'd be on
Good Morning America.

Did I hear you say, Fish gone fishin?
That's my husband. His name is Fish.

What does he like to do most?

Pause. Then she and the black man
say together, HUNT!

The man goes. She turns to me,
That's my neighbor.

We have rounded a sweet corner.
I do believe we have.

I have not always told the truth in my love poems. I hear now when I read them places where I let the reader assume I was so tenderly in love, whereas in actual life I was not that so constantly, maybe just momentarily. I call it language-love, or love for the feel of those words coming through, which makes me a kind of caricature of myself and a hypocrite. I should apologize to the women involved, and hereby do. I did not love you quite as some of the poems imply. Or maybe I am being too hard on those love poems and that loving. What if I attacked my old landscape poems as well, the inner and outer sceneries. I feel differently now about those too. I loved the days and their green wet more than I did actually say. *More.* So those are untrue in another way. Maybe *momentarily* is all we ever say, that being the essential quality of love.

I have not had a waking experience of spirit, except in the sense that Whitman says is the only way to understand his *Leaves of Grass,* by what he calls *indirection,* the unnameable something felt behind and within phenomena, that gives them significance. The hazy, exploding gold that melts form in the Turner paintings I love. Music we dance to with windiness. The Heraclitean fire that Hopkins sees in nature, the "cloud-puffball, torn tufts . . . down roughcast, down dazzling whitewash . . . ." I have felt that passionate way of looking, but how does duch relate to what happens, and what we move into, when we die? Very largely, I do imagine. Love is the clearest opening into spirit, love and friendship.

A dead friend, John Seawright, told me once through a medium that it was like he had a great balcony seat now. He can see what is going on, much better than before. He alwaya loved to make connections, and the balcony seat helps with that. Jim Kilgo, my friend the great lover, with his wicked-tickled smile tells me he makes love three times a night in spirit. It was good to see him healthy, so alive and full of himself again, and he gave me something to look forward to, though I am not sure what, bodiless sex? Or some way of making love that we cannot imagine in this place of language and cornbread and D minor suites for the cello. In that same dream I put my head underwater in a lake and could see a perfect colony of animals living in harmony. Baby raccoons crawling over each other and in among them bluish, bluntfaced furry baby animals I have no name for. All of them breathing underwater with no problem, as were Jim Kilgo and I, in our soul-element. Underwater has always felt that way. Until now, I have never put my head underwater in a dream.

Jim Kilgo and I share a fascination with indigenous rock paintings. The American Indians on their high mountain retreats drew what seem to be representations of spirit. (One figure about to jump from that into this more apparent place. Another rockface is a screen where those beings stand in such dignity and silence and watch us. As I approach the end, I begin to feel the afterlife as a definite possibility. Elisabeth Kubler-Ross has spent her life in the presence of dying people. She is very confident that death is a gorgeous transitioning from this body/mind to another way of being and knowing, of laughing and making. Where unconditional love is felt enveloping us and we are reunited with those we love who have preceded us into spirit. No one dies alone, she is sure of that. Helpers and guides are always present. My mother, a day or so before she died, said that she could see her mother, and Sarah and Edith and Rich, her sisters and brother who had already died. They were there, she said, but she could not hug them yet.

In another recent dream a dead friend, Peter Thurnauer, is there. I am putting together a short radio program about how poetry and music can merge with spirit. In the seventh grade Peter Thurnauer and I invented a way to go back inside the womb, a climbing dance with our arms, entering again the source, the mother, eternity. It was daring, done right out in the open air of the quadrangle. So boldly did we enter the anteroom of spirit that no one could quite look at us doing it. The dance remained wildly beyond anyone's ken. Peter does not understand, in the dream, why he is part of this music and poetry spirit-merge program I am putting together. I explain that he has to be part of it because he devised that womb-dance with me, so now he understands. Peter wrote a poem in his last year of high school. A man on a cliff watching a ship cross the horizon. It moves out of sight. The man jumps, a silent flick of the finger, unfunny. He won the prize that year, 1955. Years later, Pete became that inexplicable suicide. These night-visitant friends come like Nicodemuses in the dark, not so much to ask anything as to remind me of essence. Call it dew. One night it *was* dew. Be born, through such an opening.

John Seawright was cooking all kinds of meat—and he a vegetarian except for barbeque—on a huge slanted grill, showing me how they were all at just the point where they could be turned one last time, pressed and sizzled, then taken off. Though it may be impossible to *feel* how it will feel when we finally shuck this gradually slowing-down trolley and move over into something more capable of unconditional love, that spatula slide-under, and turn. Or say we shed the conditions themselves and move in a new clear way, and that we enter that sometimes now, before we die. Sweat lodges, meditation, the psychic space some of Bill Stafford's poems walk us along through, what Rumi calls "positive non-being," the emptiness. We won't know exactly the methods we have used to shuffle free until we live/die through death, and get reminded how that went. Be sure, it *is* coming toward us, says dear, honest, stubbornly doubtful Kubler-Ross. And it may be helpful to know, even just intellectually, more about the crossover. So we listen to her cds and read her books and grow a little more certain that the freedom of opening out in the sky of our true self really will come with our death that slides us into some hilarious ecstasy. And maybe it is morbidly ridiculous to *speculate* about that which will come soon and surprisingly enough, erasing all theory with its wide plain we walk out on the night of. Ding-ding, I am dead, and you are left with a big blank sheet still rolled inside the tube. Nobody knows, so we both wait for what next you may say in response, with the daring of your momentous voice, your laughter and music, spirit being so *inside* those. It may be we are each a music, and that is not just a metaphor. My friend Andrew, years ago, had a Sitka spruce fall on him in Alaska. He went out of his body and saw his crushed self under the log, and as he was moving toward the light and lightness, he heard a little tune, a melody he wanted to find an ending for, but to do that, he had to go back into the broken body. That's what he *chose* to do . . . bah dah dum dah dah doodah . . . . He jumped back in.

We dream of the dead, but it does not feel as though we make them up. More like they come on their own. By one's seventies, so many friends have died. Bur Moreland never appeared in dream while he was alive, and in this one it seems so clear that he is moving in a quality of where he is, where we all are. He is driving my ex-wife Kittsu and me in an open sleigh at night. It is snowing, a dry-crunchy, big-flake snow. He drives us laughingly up and down the old hill we love. There is no *time* in the deep quiet of slow, thick-falling snow, the three of us exultant, so *with* each other, so way more than forgiving. Spirit may be an unsayable part of the suchness everywhere, inside and out. I best be quiet like the snow about the whole thing.

Jim Hitt showed me how to love language, because he did that so well, how it could be good enough, almost, to be equal to this astonishing life. He is showing me his letters, beautifully printed, with a lavender leather cover: he is very full of love, so intelligent and mildly tickled. That was in a dream *after* he died. In real life he talked like a god holding forth with grand gesture, dance steps. Just before he died, he had a stroke and lost language. Nobody told me. They were honoring him. He was in a wheelchair. I went and knelt beside him, confiding how nobody should have to endure this sort of ceremony. He couldn't reply or laugh like he always had. At the final moment as his wheelchair rolls past me, he does his mouth open and makes a noise like *Cohhlemahhn.*

A row of synchronous flag-lions paw together at the spirit blowing through them. Pennington suddenly sits up on his deathbed. *I am here to testify.* After some time writing, or reading, in the late afternoon, I walk out with nothing to do but look up at the sky, nowhere to go but round the yard and down the street toward the sunset, bits of snow sifting indirectly onto my face, March 7th. Ways of being open to spirit and open to the work of this world; could we please be ore in cahoots with the immaterial beings we are connected to through these bodies, those we found and find again. It is as though these dead friends had asked me, before they died, if it would be helpful for me if they came back in my dreams, thus to show me how, and that they were still around in a new form of mystery similar to the one I knew them in, and that I had told them *Yes, I would appreciate that. Thank you.*

... in winter enjoy.

Blake

Late winter afternoon sliding by in silence. This delight of reading Bill Merwin's *Purgatorio*, the notes especially. The text being sometimes so settled in the politics of Dante's Florence I lose interest. I find a mistake. A note for Canto X should read 2nd Samuel, not 2nd Kings. The passage when David dances before the ark. Dante says that David's dancing makes him both less and more than a kind, a condition we have no single word for, the fool in his glory.

I was given a word in a dream recently, *frontiseratory*. I move to a dictionary, then know something else for sure, that I can be given a word in a dream, but I cannot look it up. Though I can and do when I wake, in a Latin glossary. *Frontis*, the face, the forehead, the emblem across from the title page, what is apparent to others that I cannot see, what I can know with blunt fingers. This naked device, this guidon I carry through town to draw sidewards across a pillow.

There is a lot of attention to face and forehead in the *Purgatorio*, the most beautiful being at the end of Canto I when Virgil spreads out his hands and lays them on the grass that is soaked wet with dew. Dante sees what his friend is about and leans his face near to let Virgil wash the tear stains and restore the color which their journey through hell has drained. I want a friend like Virgil to wash and restore my face with hands dipped in cold sopping fresh dew. I have had in the past such friendship walking with me through the smoke. Now pure absence looms like wisdom that wears this form out as it tries to find and give others these ablutions.

Let the reader make now the familiar two-handed gesture of wiping his or her face in a cleansing release from wherever we just were—near-sleep, prayer, reading, the leaning-back of a winter afternoon. So this then is purgatory, where we finally weep to be purified and begin to become the empty expanse we see is next.

Looking for the phrase *egotistical sublime*
in Keats' letters, hoping for a new way
to attack myself. He was giving a slap
to Wordsworth's verbosity, which I accept
as my own, deciding every time now
I am in a bookstore, I'll carry home a poet
I ought to know but don't. Marianne Moore,
Robinson Jeffers. Lord Weary. The mind *is*
an enchanting thing.
                              Rabindranath Tagore
would go off by himself for months
to a houseboat in Kashmir to read and write.
One night reading Benedetto Croce by candle,
he blew out the flame and lay there
letting his eyes get used to the dark,
and the full moon's other kind of light
magnified by its sublimation on lakewater
rose around him in bed like the extinguished mind.

At a Sunday night supper, September 28, 1890, Whitman is talking with friends. He pauses with a piece of chicken on his fork suspended between the four of them around a square table.

Leaves of Grass can never be understood except by indirection. Pauses again. It stands for that something back of phenomena, which gives it all of its significance, yet cannot be described—which eludes definition, yet is the most real thing of all.

He puts the bite in his mouth and chews and moves on to another subject. Horace Traubel was one of those there, and the notes he took on the times he spent with Whitman during Whitman's last year are published in a number of volumes called *Walt Whitman in Camden.*

I am reading this remembered bit of monologue in a cafeteria booth when a black man about my age, late 60s, walks by and stops, looking down at my plate of chicken bones. That chicken been on hard times. He waits for my response to this generosity. I say, Yeah. He's about had all the fun he's going to have.

He turns and goes, laughing. I love that human trait of turning and laughing, then walking away without further verbal reply, implying that's all this moment needs.

The short poems of a man drinking wine
are considered moving if the poet is Chinese
and out in a boat after midnight twelve hundred years ago,
and they are. It is wonderful we have any record
of the moment of a tipsy man named Po Chu-i
reading poetry in a boat by lamplight.

> *I pick up your scroll of poems and read one aloud.*
> *The poem ends, the lamp gutters, sky not yet light.*

> *My eyes hurt. I put out the lamp and go on sitting*
> *in the dark: the sound of the waves blown by headwinds*
> *sloshing against the boat.*

Yuan was the friend he was reading, as I am,
sitting in my study after three a.m.
drinking an Australian merlot,
as someone else will be in 3181, listening

to the heartbreaking friendship of poets,
unless by then we have managed to snuff out
the joy of floating and hearing a poem
making its unique sound against the boat
under the half-lit sky before dawn.

> *If I don't do Zen meditation to wipe out deluded thoughts*
> *then I must pace around drunkenly, spouting crazy songs.*

> *Otherwise in the autumn moon, or with these evenings*
> *of spring breeze, how am I to bear the idle*
> *longing for the past that comes through me?*

*   *   *

That's Po Chu-I "Forcing Myself
to Drink." I could read another called
"Tied up for the Night in a Cove,"
but I'll put a cork on it and go upstairs
to sleep with the tao of poetry under my boat.

In a restaurant near Peggy's Cove, Nova Scotia, an old man takes tiny stroke-steps going table to table. Watch out for that saw. It'll cut your head off. The crosscut blade on the wall above my head, a lumbering theme. Next table. Did you quit drinking yet? A man says, I know you. Twenty years ago in Colorado you had a boat rental place. I did. Small world. Where do you live now? Where do I live now. I don't know. Everyone laughs. The two women he's with, equally as old, come out of the restroom. It's still the same day, he says. Where do we live? Fort Payne. Twenty years. I didn't recognize you with your teeth in. He shuffles out having held high-spirited, clairvoyant conversation with all in the dining area. Now he shows us how to exist, jimdandy in the midst of menace. The three take their eternity to get to the car, then the getting in, and the floating slowly from the parking lot. He waves from the backseat like a baby, like a king in exile, like the founder of a myth-reenactment pageant inside the iron turtle of enough time.

In the late 1940s my father took me along on his summer trips to various headmaster association meetings in New England, he and I driving north through Knoxville, Kingsport, Roanoke, Washington, New York, Hartford. I loved maps. I was nine, ten, eleven. Surely he would rather have gone on those trips alone, but it was part of the psychology strategies recommended to my parents, I found out later, to help me get over my stammering, which back then and maybe now too, was thought to be connected with Oedipus. Having too easily won my mother in the family drama, I unconsciously feared my father's anger, and that nervous tension stuck in my throat, strangling language, the theory goes. On those long summer drives he and I got to be traveling buddies, his hat on the back of his head, taking it easy. I would wander whatever campus we were on, exploring, like Trinity University in Hartford. I grew up on a campus and have always felt at home in the gothic archways and amongst the boxwood of campi. Or he would put me on a tour bus or a boat around Manhattan, and get some couple to keep and eye on me. I loved the whole thing—the Smithsonian, god, I could have lived in there. The old blacktop roads led out of Chattanooga on the way to seeing the world with my dad, looking down at the map, then up at the skyline of New York across tall mudflats cattails. Neither of us knew then or now what the other was carrying: guilt, ecstasy, humiliation, glory, impotence, his terror at the sight of his brother Charles' ears and nose exploding in strokeblood, coming up the stairs toward him. I love my father and the way he took me with him, so I could soak up who he was and how well he meant by me, the two of us sitting together on the front seat day after August day in what surely is one of the *true* ways we have to help each other. What we talk about is hardly it. This good deep silence shared in the sympathetic hum of our spinal columns. I still feel his quietness nearby, dead since 1971, his half-smile, the cigar smoke. *Hey bud.*

Mr. Penny sat me on a big dining hall table carried outdoors under the three-hundred-year-old oak tree in front of forty playcampers aged four to six. I was nine. This was summer, 1946. I had gone behind the green storage cabinet and put on the fake-nose-glasses-eyebrows he had gotten somewhere and a tall hat. He introduces me as Professor Dumwhistle, who can answer any question. And I do, suddenly much goofier and more confident, wilder than any way I have ever been in my short, shy, hesitant, stammering life. I did not recognize it then, but it was a ploy, part of a number of tremendously sweet efforts that my parents and others on top of that hill made, to help me break through my speech difficulties. None of them worked—not the stammering pills, not the hypnosis by Dr. Polgar, not the black butterfly ink-blotches—nothing loosened my spring-source, my sounding out into this melodious, commodious, ventricular vehicle, this burble of rivering grace conducted over the earth by multiple amplification systems, this bass viol of tenderness and pretension. Nothing did any good, until sex took hold and gave me tongue. When I began to swim naked at night with naked girls my age, cool thigh on warm thigh sliding through, a luminous chrisming coal, a moon, a nude synonym, a ruby-lit grape, a berry on its waggly stem, touched and opened my mouth to flame, a wand within a cone, a ridged hallway to the other world. Dumwhistle is no longer a professor, though at seventy we hear he is active in retirement, a moderately well-known minor poet, traveling mystic, out-of-body facilitator, party guest, sufferable clairvoyant, and occasional sperm donor.

(bird whistling)

Dumwhistle's whistle is no longer dumb. His unruly eyebrows have become real. They zigzag out of his very brain. He walks on top of speckled daylight on the ground like a medium-sized bird. He has no tableseat of crazy wisdom, no answers, and he wears no hat.

Once in the middle of love for a woman. She is going away for three months, telling me not to worry. I am weeping, waiting for her to come back from the city where she is a lover of another, with her fidelity to two, country mouse and city mouse. I do not want to be a hermit, though I do want more moments of clear perception that living alone brings. She says there is no way to control any of this. We lie down with our shoes off. This is the way we clean house, inside a fierce, changing music. I am growing old and still delight to learn something out of an encyclopedia. I have a confused heart and no set aesthetic. There are dances I have never tried, lounging in a scrounge of watchfulness, with no private life, more a mid-region like a theatre auditorium or a restaurant, where I perform in the aisles and then the parking lot. These winter skies, I can almost imagine living with one of them, inside the buckling we call *kneeling*, with evening birdbits distributing themselves. Seedsound in a cold diamond, the superb ache when a few hours of writing begin.

I would like to hear what you have escaped, how you slipped free from some compulsion or inherited conditioning. What moves your story along? Tangents, errands, resupply. Desire, absence of desire, partial fulfillment. Galway Kinnell says that, at seventy-seven, desire is still to him the most beautiful thing. I would rather some fluency come, useful-ness and a longed-for spontaneity. Robert Graves to the very end was writing love poems for his muses, women with muse-potential, always on the lookout for new ones. I have heard people dismiss those late love poems as silly, not appropriate for the elder, the great shaman. But it is those poems that feel most alive to me, unburdened by thought, so lightly set loose, a tissue, barely there.

Before conscious memory, before language
gave me these unsatisfactory terms
for saying who I am and how emotions
are flowing through, everything
I had to lose was whole.

Now I am sixty-nine, full of doubt-fragments
of rage and tenderness,
and I have had a vision of frightening
forgetfulness, a dream
on August 11.

This is how it goes. I am in an urban conference
setting, walking in and out
of wide hallways and those huge meeting rooms
with adjustable walls.

I am confused and have no short-term memories
to locate myself with. It is a very convincing sense
of how it may feel to have had a stroke.

Then I am in a car, driving,
with a man in the passenger seat talking.

I have no recall as to who he is, how we got here,
or what he is talking about. I am driving,
going nowhere that I know.

Now in the dream I am seated at a table
of restored consciousness
with this awareness we have here,
the connection to time and space,
with this sharing through the eyes

a knowledge of who we are, and where,
and a few ingenious guesses as to why.

Such beautiful companionship
holds that table of bright being.

A man at the other end, a friend in the spirit,
no one known actually, he looks at me
seeing the grief and terror I have just felt
for my diminished consciousness.

He reaches his hand toward me acknowledging the grief.
I hold his fingers. That was the dream.

Now at another table, not in any dream,
a round restaurant table. I come along an aisle.
They see me first
and put paper napkins up to hide their faces
except for the eyes, like muslim women,
like harem princesses, like train robbers.

It is my son Benjamin, 42, and his two children,
Briny, 14, and Tuck, 7.
I sit down and tell them the dream.
Then announce that I shall recite
an Emily Dickinson poem that I have just last night
memorized, proof I have not lost it yet.

God made a little gentian.

I explain what they may not know
that a gentian is a blue flower that blooms
in late November. Some of them grow
in a little dell near my cabin.

At the appointed time each year I go out,
as a poet must, and there they are,

deep imperial blue, the size
of Christmas bulbs glowing.

    God made a little gentian.
    It tried to be a rose and failed.
    And all the summer laughed.
    But just before the snows

    There rose a purple creature
    That ravished all the hill,
    And summer hid her forehead
    And mockery was still.

Pause, longpause.

    The frosts were her condition.

That's the best line.
So far, yes it is, says Briny.

Now I lose the thread completely
of the poem's going.

    The frosts were her condition.

Pause. I am very close to cursing
in front of my grandchildren.

    God made a little gentian, I repeat.

    God made a little snowman, says Benjamin.
    Frosty was his name, says Tuck.

    His nose was drippy and his eyes
    were cruel and insane, says Briny.

• • •

They're going round the table.

He romped and played the tuba.
No one could keep him quiet.

They sent him to Aruba
And put him on a rice diet.

Grow still thy mockery,
I chime in grand poetic tone.

So I shall now paraphrase
what I cannot precisely
at this moment quote.

The lady would not put on her purple dress,
until this relative from up North called,
somewhere near Chicago, to suggest
she should get out more, join a book club
or learn French. No need to be chained
to an apartment like a park bench to a pole.

Now the Tyrian, ah the Tyrian from Tyre,
it comes back, ancient coastal town
down where now is brutal Lebanon.

Tyre and Sidon, twin sources
for the beach mollusk dye
so prized by royalty, indigo
with streaks of crimson.

The Tyrian would not come,
and why should she, really.

* * *

The Tyrian would not come
until the North invoke it.

Wait for it, wait,
Emily's poignant final question,
so late arising in November.

Creator, shall I bloom?

Thus to openly satirize Granddaddy
loudly and unanimously,
when he shall more obviously
be losing it than now

may be a way to finish dinner
without having to sit in silence
while he weeps for his forgetting

God's goddam little gentian
that nobody can remember how
or where he used to put it.

This is not the end.
We shall use the gentian
for a blue flower torch
through the dark of this
into whatever is next.

The sky's deep blue before it goes black,
darkest dew-soaked shade, my friend,
this love at the last
that does not want to leave.

Even with time no longer in the mix,
we grow more awake in the night of it,
this lovelike lake filling with snowmelt.

I would love to make out with you.

My best friend.

All he does is get drunk.

I would love to get him drunk. I will buy him drinks all night long.

I am so sweet you would not believe.

I just want to sleep with him, but he won't let me touch him.

Darlin. Ashby. You have to do it subtly.

If I was his girl, I'd be home with him right now. It would be like bye y'all,

It's getting stormy outside.

Shut up.

I wear clothes that fit my body type.

I don't like this outfit. I want to go change.

Nooooo. No.   No.

If you say can I buy you a shot, he'll take it. You have to be direct. I have money. Keep buying.

Where is everybody?

Everybody's gone next door trying to get laid.

. . .

Stormy's like covered.

If you're looking for a brother, that he's not.

I would be all, I mean, all over her. Really.

I love my girlfriend.

Y'all going to get married?

Potato pancakes.

You can wait with me.

Not that Tommy, the one that works at Dino's.

What do you think?

I am so invisible. They cannot possibly. Here they come.

I love you.

I love you too.

Will you marry me?

If you have a ring.

I can get one.

You work on that.

President Bush, before you order airstrikes,
imagine the first cruise
missile as a direct hit on your closest friend.

That might be Laura. Then twenty-five other
family and friends.
There are no survivors. Now imagine some

other way to do it. Quadruple the inspectors.
Put a thousand and one
U.N. People in. Then call for peace activists

to volunteer to go to Iraq for two weeks each.
Flood that country with
well-meaning tourists, people curious about

the land that produced the great saints, Gilani,
Hallaj, and Rabia.
Set up hostels near those tombs. Encourage peace

people to spend a bunch of money in shops, to bring
rugs home and samovars
by the bushel. Send an Arabic translator with

every four activists. The U.S. government will pay
for the translators and for
building and staffing the hostels, one hostel for

every twenty visitors and five translators. Central
air and heat are state of the art,
and the hostels belong to the Iraqis at the end

. . .

of this experiment. Pilgrims with carpentry skills
will add studios, porches,
armadas, meditation cribs on the roof, clerestories,

and lots of subtle color. Jimmy Carter, Nelson
Mandela, and my friend,
Jonathan Granoff at the U.N., will be the core

organizational team. Abdul Aziz Said too has got
to be in on this, who
grew up in a Bedouin tent four hundred miles

east of Damascus. He didn't see a table until
he was fourteen. Shamans
from various traditions, Martin Prechtal,

Bly, and many powerful women, Sima Simar,
Debra, Naomi, Jane.
I offer these exalted services without having

asked anybody. No one knows what might come
of such potlatch, potluck.
Maybe nothing, or maybe it would show some

of the world that we really do not wish to kill
anybody and that we
truly are not out to appropriate oil reserves.

We're working on building a hydrogen vehicle
as fast as we can, aren't we?
Put no limit on the number of activists from all

over that might want to hang out and explore Iraq
for two weeks. Is anything
left of Babylon? There could be informal courses

*   *   *

for college credit and pickup soccer games every
evening at five. Long,
leisurely, late suppers. Chefs will come for cookouts.

The U.S. government furnishes air transportation,
that is, hires airliners from
the country of origin and back for each peace tourist,

who must carry and spend the equivalent of $1001
U.S. inside Iraq. Keep part
of the invasion force nearby as police, but let those

who claim to deeply detest war try something else
just this once, for one year.
Call our bluff. Medical services, transportation

inside Iraq, along with many other ideas that
will be thought of later
during the course of this innocently, blatantly

foolish project will all also be funded by
the U.S. Government. But what
if terrible unforeseen disaster rains down

because of this spontaneous, unthought-out
hippie notion? One
never knows. Surely it wouldn't be worse

than the *shock and awe* display we have planned
for the first forty-eight hours.
But we must always suspect intentionally good

deeds. Consider this more of a lark, a skylark.
Look. There is
a practice known as *sema*, the deep listening

* * *

to poetry and music, with sometimes movement
involved. Unpremeditated
art and ease. We could experiment with whole

nights of that, staying up till dawn, sleeping
in tents during the day.
Good musicians will be lured with more than

modest fees. Cellos, banjos, oboes, ouds,
French horns. Hundreds
of harmonicae and the entire University

of North Carolina undergraduate gospel choir.
Thus, instead of war,
there is much relaxed, improvisational festivity

from March 2003 through February 2004. It could be
as though war had already
happened, as it has. And now we're in the giddy,

brokenopen aftertime. So let slip the pastel
minivans of peace and whoa
be they who cry surcease. I'll be first to

volunteer for two weeks of wandering winter desert,
reading Hallaj, Abdul Qadir
Gilani, dear Rabia, and Scheherazade's life-prolonging

thousand and one *Arabian Nights*. I am Coleman Barks,
retired English professor eee-
meritus, living in Athens, Georgia, and I don't

really consider this proposal foolish. More brash
and hopeful for the bunch
I come along with, those born from the mid-1920s

•   •   •

until the mid-1940s, that before we die or lose
our energy, we might,
with help from tables, sitar, waterwheeling

sixteen-strings, and the pulsing voices of seventy
black-church-bred students push away
from terrorism and cruise missile terrorism

and the video-techno-laser, loveless, unerotic-
idiotic, bio-chemo atom-toys,
and decide not to study war so much no more.

Never denying we have the tendencies built-in,
a cold murderous
aggression, a who-cares-it's-all-bullshit-

anyway turning away from those in pain.
March 15th, 2003, and I am
not quite yet weary enough of words not to try

to say the taste of this failure we sponsor
with our tax dollars,
but after the stupidity starts, I might be.

Shams Tabriz says
if the Kaaba were suddenly lifted up
out of this world, we would see
that in five-times prayer
each of us is bowing to the other,
everyone to every other.

No need for forms of worship.
Take religion out of the picture.
Let friendship be openly
what it already is.

The scrapwood man in Shiraz
has a onefoot square, makeshift table
that he saws larger pieces
into kindling on with a hacksaw.

He looks up at us as we pass,
puts the table and saw aside,
and holds out both arms
to us, smiling.

No language. He has no words
from any word-lineage anymore.

He gestures toward a bulletin board
of pictures, photos of himself
in younger years, very alive and charismatic.
He looks like the young Meher Baba.

* * *

Irregular woodfruit pieces
hang about the shallow storefront.

We stop and put our hands
across our chests and bow,
but we do not stay.

We could have sat down on the sidewalk
and let him show us how to accept
unwanted wood from neighbors,
how to cut it to a proper length,
then bind those into bundles for the fires
that people on this street
are apt to make.

So it continues as a grief
and a brightening mistake,
that I often do not forsake
the habitual to accept the company
of the scrapwood man's eyes.

———————————

Another refusal, a continuing on
that is a turning away,
not from wordless conversation,
but from brave talking.

This with the grace I am given
time to be in the presence of,
Bawa Muhaiyaddeen.

Early in those nine years,
maybe on the second day,
I was leaving, going to the airport,
back home, on the landing
coming down from the upstairs bedroom

where he received visitors and talked
sitting crosslegged on his bed.

He came to the top railing and called.
Did I want to have some private time
with him? I waved the opportunity
away, saying I'll be coming back.

Is it fear of meeting the nakedest core,
the one who knows all my secrets,
where they come from, where they lead?

I never brought it up, talking with him
afterward. The denial was such
I just now remember it.

I want to go back, still frightened
by the scalding, icy springwater,
up that half-flight of stairs.

I have skirted the edge
of disintegration, edge
of union, on the teasing curl
of something evermore about to be,
as Wordsworth said of April.
Close, but no *fana.*

I see the failure of courage,
failure to be fully alive,
my characteristic failure,
not to respond with full spontaneity,
generosity, fearless imagination,
openhearted confession, whatever
consciousness I might muster,
without holding back.

* * *

I have often avoided
the wholehearted *yes*
saying there is plenty
of time. There is not.

Think about it some. Take it easy.
That is the continuous advice
of the cowardly *nafs*
that want things not to change.

What I want is the moment
on the landing again.

Best quit wanting
a wistful impossibility.
Accept the friendship I have.

I was riding in a car in Minneapolis
last November with a nun, Irene O'Neill,
who told me that a spirit-seeing woman
saw a small dark man with me
during my reading at Pax Christi.
Then she saw he was inside me.

I wonder what is true.
Let me not move away
too quickly ever again
from the scrapwood man.

FROM *TENTMAKING* (2002)

Bill Pettway came to visit the other night,
and there were four walls of water
pouring down into a square cistern

where he was showing me
how our lives are one volume in constant revision,
language being always altered,

and how revisions overlap and duplicate
each other, as some revisions I was bringing
were already being made.

Then the realization in the dream
that Pettway was dead. He died suddenly
several years ago heaving lumber

into the back of a truck. My memories of him
go back to kindergarten when he did
the most daring criminal act anyone ever considered.

He threw scissors off the balcony
where some of us were doing art
down into the area where the rest of us were.

I imagine he remembers doing that in the place
he comes to my dreams from. Now the maroon squares
of the kindergarten floor come clear,

where cots were put out for our afternoon naps.
And this: I slept longer and deeper
than anyone, and the wonder is they let me.

. . .

Each afternoon to wake and be the only cot there
in the big room. Maybe the janitor
would still be carrying and stacking the canvas cots

in the hall, or maybe he had finished and gone.
That aloneness stays inside me
like an afternoon. Like summer turning night

and lightning bugs, their beauty floating my height
in a hollow of black locust, oak,
and hickory, some higher in the branches.

The point is *not* to put them in a jar
where they clump and quit winking and next morning
smell of exhausted phosphor.

Leave the lovers of scintillae in the air
they love, gracing distance
with their dance. Pettway was telling me

that every moment contains the dead, and they are not
dead, but doing this revision with us.
And that I should get my revisions out *quicker.*

I was keeping them in my mind too long.
At the end he began speaking a Borneo dialect,
which appeared in script to the side,

Oolek bineng weresak, not that exactly but similar.
And the next night new Ohio poems
by James Wright came, a canoe seen from above,

the line of its motion in the river behind it
briefly. Wright and Bly were helping me
teach a poetry class. Pettway was there

• • •

with his mouth open in an O. His nickname
through highschool was Puss.
He dated Jean Carter, whose pale and freckled

redheaded body kindled my desire for women early
on the bank of Chickamauga Lake
lying under the full moon pouring its wrinkling

waterpath to us. Then the freckling on her legs
became a vine design one could somehow drink
and slake desire for those legs, for a time.

Time and time words build their contradiction.
Call it *tentmaking*; one twists rope;
another carves wooden pegs; someone weaves;

there is a man stitching and one tearing cloth.
Reprobate and righteous, loyal and dis;
provoker, provoked. We cannot help but do this

we are. This is, and even if we could see
the purpose, still no one's faith
would increase. Every act is praise, no matter.

I know a man who was standing in a long line
for a movie with a huge amount of coins
in his pockets, hundreds of nickels, dimes,

quarters, pennies. He suddenly spills all
to the sidewalk and changes everything: stiff
and separate people bend and gather,

helping, laughing, stealing. They throw
handfuls into the grassy medians
of the parking lot; saying becomes rolling coinage.

• • •

We are nothing but some seeing that includes
those who have died: desire and collective editing:
a wooden truckload, this river of roots

where a golden-legged lover builds a tent
of cover and her body over me. We talk
inside this word-wet hearing-fog we breathe.

The internet says science is not sure
how cats purr, probably
a vibration of the whole larynx,
unlike what we do when we talk.

Less likely, a blood vessel
moving across the chest wall.

As a child I tried to make every cat I met
purr. That was one of the early miracles,
the stroking to perfection.

Here is something I have never heard:
a feline purrs in two conditions,
when deeply content and when
mortally wounded, to calm themselves,
readying for the death-opening.

The low frequency evidently helps
to strengthen bones and heal
damaged organs.

Say poetry is a human purr,
vessel mooring in the chest,
a closed-mouth refuge, the feel
of a glide through dying.

One winter morning on a sunny chair,
inside this only body,
a far-off inboard motorboat
sings the empty room, urrrrrrrhhhh
                    urrrrrrrhhhhh
                    urrrrrrrhhhhh

Our game is to lower a fluffing riffle
of dictionary pages held dangling
by the front and back covers,

its fingertip toeholds slowly up and down
and across my erect penis
pointing to the ceiling to see what word

its tip nudges into notice: *pathos,*
the ache that suffers through the fingers,
then *pendulous.* Your breasts

take hold and words go blurry inside
the *smoor* of where they point.

I cannot help claiming we have found
a way to honor at one time two loves,
for language and the body, though clearly
more research is indicated.

Be met at the suite door, deprived
of handheld items, discalced
by one already kneeling,

unsocked, your sweet-smelly feet caressed
and pinktoenailed toes cleaned in between
with a wet cloth and tickled. Arch, heel,
and ankle footwashed like an early Christian.

Now sit and let your pants be pulled, shirt
unbuttoned, bra and panties tossed
into tomorrow. Diswrist watch,

leaving only Kwan Yin at the greenwhirling
center, for I too am naked who lead you
to the perfect shower and soap

your Corinthian shoulders and breasts
and knees and neck and Cappadocian me
and rub you Smyrna priestess dry and me

and walk us tottering Mesopotamians
to bed to schmooz and kiss and writhe
and curl inside the creamy filling.

When time comes sliding back—a truck
gears down outside—we will go
somewhere that's open and eat.

I know you love me. You love my eyes.
You love my eyes looking in your eyes
with our love and all.

Sometimes you want to pound me
with your tiny beautiful fists
and your insistent, skinny,
so-sensitive undersided, forearms.

This will all go away—my eyes, your skin,
what we so love and the energy
of their beauty, the parts.

My question is not when.
Let that sequence be. I even claim
that some of my love for you
will go right through the ornate wooden panel
of dying. I feel the wholeness of it will.

Oh I have no question. I thought I did,
but I don't. Do. You that love
the erotic stars and paperclips,
will I have to watch you making love
with a man other than me? Poor me.

I watch you near me, in you, so sweetly.
Will I have to hear your moans mix with
another's mouth making the chorale of spring?

Will you have to hear mine?
I feel sad asking this, but I do
with some courage ask. And answer
my side of it no and I don't know.

   .   .   .

But living-hearing the synchronous music
of this friendship is so much the ordinary air
being breathed, it would feel unnatural
not to be that word I have rarely used,
faithful, yours.

Peeper, shall we consider unasked
what never could be answered anyway?

With poignant howl and undergrumble
the sentimental nightly train leaves empty.
A light waggle to the line of cars
is how I guess.

I love the tentative balance
of this wild devotion, our urgent hungering
with meditation, this evening walk
I invite you for.

Notebooks handy to the sudden phrase,
a green glove, your hand on my wrist.

Tomorrow is Candlemas, the day of the dead,
how they stay and what they care about,
no longer ask of, how they see
and visit our shawl of silence
as a small wind spirals flame.

Grateful for what's given,
not always able to bear it,
going out.

They say the best French wines have *terroir*, meaning the taste of the lay of the land that works through and gets held in the wine, the bouquet of a particular hillside and of the care of those who work there.

When I see Bill Matthews coming along, I see and taste the culture of the world, a lively city, a university campus during Christmas break, a few friendly straggling scholars and artists. I taste the delight of language and desire and music. I see a saint of the great impulse that takes us out at night, to the opera, to the ballgame, to a movie, to poetry, a bar of music, a bar of friends.

When I see Bill Matthews stopped at the end of a long hall, I see my soul waiting for me to catch up, patient, demanding, wanting truth no matter what, the goofiest joke, the work with words we are here to do, saying how it is with emptiness and changing love, and the unchanging. Now I see his two tall sons behind him.

Bill would not say it this way; he might even start softly humming Amazing Grace if I began my saying, but I go on anyway: god is little g, inside out, a transparency that drenches everything you help us notice: a red blouse, those black kids crossing Amsterdam, braving the cabs, a nun. You sweet theologian, you grew new names for god: gourmet, cleaning woman, jazz, spring snow.

What fineness and finesse. I love Bill Matthews, and I did not have near enough time walking along with him, talking books and ideas, or sitting down to drink the slant and tender face of Provence.

Late one Thursday afternoon I arrive in Vermont from Georgia. I have been invited to the Bennington campus to give three lectures on "The Natures and Uses of Ecstatic Poetry." That night I dream of people in south India throwing a ball back and forth across an ampitheatre with steep seats. They are very adept at throwing and catching a blue ball, smaller than a volley ball, larger than a softball.

I give my first lecture in a room with steep seats, and afterward talking on the phone with my friend, Judith Orloff, I tell her the dream. She gets an intuitive hit that I should mention the word ball in my second lecture. *Promise me you will.*

Walking the campus later, I think to buy a ball, but where, in the bookstore? Since I would be talking next about playfulness in poetry, I could toss it around and involve the audience. The sun was going down, and the new moon was coming up as that idea broke through at the top of a rise on the path to my guest house. It was the new moon signaling the end of Ramadan, a traditionally auspicious moment.

A few steps further on where the path dips beside a pond, I see a black rubber ball. Almost in the center of the walkway. I pick it up with amazed gratitude and put it to good use in the next lecture. It turns out an audience's attention sharpens considerably when there is the possibility a ball might be thrown to anyone at any moment.

I am surprised and honored to see Mary Oliver in the audience. She teaches part of the year at Bennington and to my mind is the greatest living ecstatic poet. She comes up and pulls on my sleeve. *I left that ball for you.* She was walking her dogs, Ben and Bear, and left that black rubber ball behind. It was not her dogs' toy. She saw it over in the grass and brought it to the path for whoever might come by.

* * *

All this before I had the idea. She did not have me especially in mind, but I was chosen, blackballed. And now I use this Greek instrument for ostracizing to show how playfully intelligent the web of connections is we live. The 13th-century mystic Rumi says form itself is ecstatic: being shaped and sentient a state of pure rapture.

Follow the bouncing ball and sing along as we used to at the Saturday movies. I carry it with me now whenever I give readings. Consider how like an ecstatic poem it is, this ball. Resilient. Agent of spontaneous friendship with strangers. Adored of dogs, lovingly chewed up, it kisses the ground and springs away to fall and kiss again and rest in any human hand its round and subtle energy.

A dream of south India comes. I tell Judith, who has an intuition. I add to it, then find a black rubber ball on my late afternoon path. I fool around in a lecture. Mary Oliver comes up to say she was walking her dogs and left that for me. I motion you away some now, dear reader, so we can get more arc on our poised exchange, this note.

A forgotten memory came to me
while I was reading a Seamus Heaney poem
back across the Atlantic on the phone to Chloe,
a poem about when Thomas Hardy as a boy
got down on all fours among sheep
and looked in their bland faces
and tried to feel how it was to be one.

I was in the tub as a boy
when I heard my little sister coming
and pretended to be drowned,
curled under the bathwater, just an ear out
to hear her intake of breath and running
to the living room where our parents
were playing bridge with the Penningtons.

A violent sliding back of chairs,
adult feet pounding. I go back under
to my drowned self: am translated dripping,
giving my naked foolery smile, like a dog
lifted up to wave bye-bye.

The bridge players spank and hug me both.
The hand must be redealt, bids forgotten.
Mr. Penny howling, *It's a miracle, gollee,
he rose from the dead, O slow of heart,*
take down this to read
when I do actually die, no fooling.

Nothing can save us. This sweetness dies and rots.
Luke was a thirty-year-old pharmacy graduate
student who worked at Horton-Add Drugs,
at the post office in the back
that stays open until seven p.m., my p.o.

It also has a lunch counter.
He sometimes did things behind there,
like make me a tuna fish sandwich
and fill a glass with ice and diet coke.

He mopped the place and swept up,
as quick and accurate with the broom-jabs
as he was at calculating my strange Tasmanian mail.
Hey, Finland! Once I sent out seventy-four books
priority mail. He said, It looked like Christmas
back there. In the storeroom where
the mailman picks up.

He laughed so easily with his quiet industry,
something out of Norman Rockwell.
He's maybe the most promising thing we are,
Luke, young American man just before
he meets a woman and raises a family
and does church group and Little League,
and every good thing stored in his strong hands
comes building out into the air.
Luke, master of small fixing.

Now on the glass double door, this handwritten
posterboard for his memorial service.
11 a.m. today. I missed it.

Would I have gone? *Luke Poucher.*
I never knew a last name.

One day we had some talk about how he knew
my name from all the mail, but I didn't know
his. Luke. That's a great name.

He was killed instantly last Thursday
in an automobile accident down the street
on Lumpkin at Old Princeton Road,
where he lived, not half a mile from me,
not a week ago. I had not heard
and don't now ask the Horton family for details.

Car wreck. Luke's dead. Luke 17:12.
The kingdom of God is within you.
He was so lightheartedly that,
it took your breath.

Is it with his death I fear my own
before the loving here gets as open
as it might could get in such as me?

I do not understand Dylan Thomas' "Refusal
to Mourn the Death of a Child
by Fire in London."

After the first death, there is no other,
he concludes, but on what authority?
He pictures his own death as entering
again the round Zion of the water bead . . .
the synagogue of the ear of corn,
and I have loved those words
since I first heard them in 1957.

* * *

I see the holy, tiny, elemental
corridors of corn grains and the fragile
tearshape inside the word *Zion.*
He says the nameless girl who burned
to death is now with the robed dead
by the unmourning Thames.

It may be Luke is off somewhere profound
and myriad, though I feel him close
and still-mortal as I write this, waiting
for the foolish satisfaction
of my own phrasing.

What is the sudden subtraction of a young man,
who might just as well be my son,
a filament of ocean beauty
I do and don't see today, do.

I grieve the death of Luke Poucher
for the place he swept and tended so well,
this fivepointed threshing floor
of stores and walkers and apartments,
mailmen, depositors, lunching retiree,
chemo-waver, body-worker, skateboarder,
UPS, any bunch that knows each other's
half-grin in hurried irritation
out doing errands.

Let this be Luke, this end of the parking lot
around the mailboxes, Luke Poucher Place.
The air, the few flowers,
and the people as they meet going in
to buy lunch or stamps or shampoo,
their small nods of helplessness.

•   •   •

I asked for duct tape once.
You know, we ought to carry that,
but we don't. It's about all I know
how to do to fix anything.

I've got some broken ducks.
I need to get them in a row.

Let this low talking, the love and joking
we do fumbling for courtesy
here at the door be Luke, Luke
looking up from the stroke
of his all-hallowing broom, *Beautiful*
out there, idn't it?

John Seawright's great uncle Griff Verner
spent much of his last days whittling neck-yokes
for his chickens to wear,
so they couldn't get through the wide
slat divisions of his yard fence.

There are other possible solutions
to this problem, but eggs have yolks,
and Griff Verner's chickens had yokes,
and he himself had that joke-job
in a bemused neighborhood that watched every move.

Somewhere there is a crate of Griff's chicken yokes,
I hope, as there is a wild shoebox
of vision-songs stashed by a poet whose name
we do not know yet, nor the beauty and depth
of his soulmaking, or hers.

Griff's white pine, Rembrantian fowl-collars
may have served as handles to wring their necks
with when Sunday demanded.

John's grandmother's Methodist house
had only two books in it, the *Holy Bible,*
and Fox's *Book of Martyrs.*

When it rained, there was not much to do indoors,
and on Sundays nothing, no games,
no deck of cards, no dominoes.
Of course, no television.

.   .   .

I grew up in a house with no tv in the 1940s
and on into the mid- 50s. We were in education.
Sometimes at night there would be five
different people in four different rooms
reading five different books.

John says once his mother caught Sam and him
playing cards on the floor.
She snatched up the deck and said,
Well, you can play cards in jail.

There's always chores to do
in the methodical world, no spare time to kill.
Throw those idle gypsy two-faces in the trash.
Let them find other haphazard palms to occupy.

John's father could carry on a side conversation
with him while typing a sermon.
John remembers how as a child he would sit and talk
with his dad and watch those two word-things
simul-manu-larynxactly together
in the after-dinner Friday night office.

Griff Verner's whittling comes
when you are not spry enough to chase chickens
but still take some interest
in the public's consternation with oddness.

It is a spring morning in the 1940s
when Ozella and my mother misunderstand
each other. The exterminator man
in his green Orkin uniform coming up the walk,
mother calls from the porch
back to the kitchen, Do we have any bugs?

No'm. We used all those we had yesterday.
She had thought mother'd said bulbs,
light bulbs, mother so elongated
her buuuhhhs, and barely put
final consonants on at all.

Now here's the bug man with his metal spray gun
lying down on the brick walk to laugh.

We are so ready to laugh in the 1940s,
we get down on our sides to enjoy it.

With the light in the tree above
Jittery Joe's I am wondering about energy
exchange. The sun gives itself wholly
to the tree and us all, but the leaves
on this side get additional nighttime
attention from artificial light, whose
power derives from water falling
sixty feet off a dam to turn a turbine.

I do not know how any of this works,
least of all the cholorophyll, what
out of sunlight and earthen minerals
and magical moisture makes oak
leaves by the bushel basket.

Some exchange not unlike this
must go on between people.

The enlightened ones and the near-to,
and the goofy joyful ones and those
that dance their ignorance with those
that laugh melodious, and others
who play like roots in the dirt.

The various flavors of lightedness
take human forms and compose their waking
motions to enjoy the growing conversation.

This is a pecan, its double trunk held
by a seam in the cement. And of course,
it is like us in the midst of constant
traffic noise, how we live so fierce
and shamed and free, too busy, and lovingly
bent over with our nut-bearing gift.

With normal ignorance, I follow
this elegant ant crossing my page
before I can think of a thing.

The ballpoint falls in behind like buddies
crossing a desert. They angle up and left,
northwest, northeast off the paper,
back on and down southeast,
making a fair freehand coastline
of the north end of the Persian Gulf.

I began the line well down the western shore
from Kuwait. This was moments before
or *during* the Dhahran bombing of the American compound
that killed nineteen. About then,
I was tracking my ant, wondering *what's right there.*

He knew I was dogging him,
but stayed unalarmed, did not quicken
his pace, had a map to sketch.

A Mercedes fuel truck with a Swiss mechanism
stops at the gate. It and the getaway car
go left to an empty lot.

There is a drawing my mother made
one Tuesday afternoon in 1970 in a letter
I still have. She had seen my office
in the English department, and exclaimed
at the red oak window-companion,
holder of nest, moulder of acorn,
When the leaves come off, draw me that tree.

She does a few limbs on a central trunk.
Looks like my chest x-ray, she jokes.

The oak died and was cut down by the grounds crew.
Mother's winter diagnosis was lung cancer,
dead by May. The great mulberry flourishes
in place of the oak in my office vista.

Seven crows land on the fruiting crown
and begin idle harvest, urged
to change perch periodically by young squirrels.
Very lively scene out my unopenable
glass. The bomb: forty-eight living rooms
harpooned with shards of picture window.

Those who had gone to bed now sleep
with their shoes on. Others, the night owls,
died and are buried.

The old sink upsidedown in the backyard
prior to being hauled off to the dump,
its scummy drainage nub in the air,
makes a perfect roost for the owl
I have been glimpsing down the driveway.

Wideawake in the daytime, here is
another high-spirited omen of death.

Who can praise quickly enough
the truth of how we are here,
on a walk, or a trip to the mall
to buy a toy refrigerator, and two or three
shirts, or how with due panache
we appear on television, then each
alone in too much traffic?

*   *   *

I say we can praise quickly, if not enough.
The ant walks into my sleeping ear,
and it is inside the sun, where we sit
and laugh like Shadrach, Meshach, and Abednego,
in a furnace honeycomb of hallways
made of gold and grapeskin-glaucous light.

A night-sleeping rain
become now these puddle-windows
where we watch each other's eyes in a wet field:

how we are *not* dead and buried.
The bread-push underfoot: loved ones
in a spherical bed so wide and round
we stretch your left sole to my right
to (wicker worsa) walk as each the other's path:

waking and dream in a kiss-touch
continuum: breath-faces moving at the mirror lip
bahbah bahbahbah, as when I did observe
under the glass-skin: turtle moving moss thread,
a frog's one-eye wink, before school

or any fear of the talking-knot tightening
in my stuck throat, rather its opposite release,
what scientists call the abscission layer
circling the stem where it lets go
and begins fly-fall. The gingko

has an abscission leaf which when it goes, the rest
will not be long: her yellow slip slips
as we turn to see and feel the abscission-words
loosen: night ensuing night, their resinous balsam
carry my slow-spilled dose,

and a long river-silence flows in the juice: a red
blackspotted tupelo leaf and a yellow
fivepointed sweetgum rise off the silt floor
turning their tips to touch the surface
from the other side and sail.

.   .   .

I am lying asleep in a nightriver room
strobed with boatlight sidling the curve,
its engine throb below the cliff
boiling the churn and mix.

By the violets in the watercress
new grass under the slender ash trees
by the rooted-river spidery bankedge,

I fold in with edible, lavender butterflies,
each next each in a wandering myth
of body, and crows. I do not know who I am,

or ever will, who invite friends to see
a silo of memory, whose house
is an empty plot between an uncovered well

and this other cylinder of poured concrete.
We go clumped together as a kind of a way for a while,
then take our single stems aloof.

Listening to music in the dark, I feel
a great sphere of violets and water and grass
riding in the night between us and the moon.

It cannot be looked at directly; it is
more elusive than even our fluttering stories
that leave a silky damp in the air.

I missed giving my final final exam. I slept through it. The alarm didn't sound, or I turned it off in my sleep. I'm buying a new clock. But maybe it's perfect this way. They wrote me such letters. I'll give them all A's. But that moment will not come back, no matter how I call, howl for it to, weep. This morning will not come back this afternoon.

This class really was the best I ever, and I regret, I regret. It hurts so much missing the saying goodbye to each as they come up, my best, my last. I cannot believe I missed the final final. The predictable conclusion to my legend in the English department. The secretaries loved it. I can't believe it, and I won't say I'm sorry. I *am* sorry, like my mother used to call unreliable hired help. You can't count on him; he's just sorry. You never know if he'll show up. I'm so sorry I won't say I'm sorry.

And actually it gives me a chance to give 40 A's, which out of some arrogant, ungenerous grading attitude, I would not have done, which now I do, with an iron whang of the Grades Only chute door in the back of the Academic Building, and an illegal pull of the chapel bell.

Do you reckon I'll sleep through my death, another pull, sleep through Resurrection Day, another, and have to do this whole jabbering career again, pull, or will I get to go on to some other plane where there's no such thing as dreamless sleep and discipline and drinking too much the night before and faulty clocks and forgetfulness and the frustration of saying anything in front of groups, and no such a thing as regret and the satisfaction of a job well done, and no more ceremonial walk-through doors, and no way to miss the living moments, and no way to try and write them right.

Or say there is nothing after now. Then that lovely bunch of young people talking and laughing and writing me letters, forgiving me even, straggling out of that room made sacred by our presences and attention, were gone when I arrived at 10:45. You created quite a stir around here says someone on the hall bench. I bet. I heard them say you've used up your poetic license.

This is how death might surprise, as the thing undone, irremediably missed-out-on. You round a corner and the backyard party with your friends is breaking up. Where have you been! Alone, asleep. If I lived with someone, I might have been jogged awake, reminded, but I still don't want to live with anyone.

I am unrepentantly, sufficiently, some would say terribly, alone. Look at me and be frightened of not pouring the last of the love and wakefulness you're given, which is every moment, but moreso some than others. Emptying out is the point. In time, over time, be early.

This woman currycombs
her brown stallion, Dervish,
in an open stableyard.

She pats and coos and rubs and traces
muscle-thread from haunch to knee,
shoulder to hip, radiating each thew,
ear-rim, lash, moaning into the huge raked
and roiling body as if she were
the invisible being who supposedly
tends this world. Supposedly nothing.

She picks his sheath clean of flakes
of rotted black skin, combs and flickers
there, a common practice.

He is her doorway, where what is touched
flames and consciously mirrors back,
a conversation of leg and groin
to along and down, breezy lovers
before and after in sweetness not of
consummation, but in the whooing exchange
the dervishes call *sohbet*, one step
above meditation, which is a step up
from prayer.

She swirls the triple spiral of Newgrange,
the shape of midwinter snaking in
to wake our burial mound forehead of stone.
This woman makes that again and again
on the side of her horse.

. . .

So slip your hand
into whatever you use for a currycomb.
Feel the layered pack alive beneath words—field,
faces, hue, tone, chip, grain—the twitch
of overlapping melody as you
and your animal are talking.

Donald Hall *is* falling,
and I cannot catch him.

Not seeing the little stepdown
at the bottom of the slanted chapel aisle,
he falls in slowmotion,
to his knees, then sidewise to his shoulder.
His dear head does not hit. *I'm OK.*

There is a long getting up, three-quarters
of the audience there. He raises one hand
in mock triumph. This is the first poetry reading
of his eighth decade, magnificent, tender,
broken open with naked grief.

Afterward, after the signing and the jokes
and the serious student advice,
he and I sit beaming our eyes at each other,
side by side at the Holiday Inn bar.

What I most loved about the night was
that from the fall to now,
I took his arm with both my hands
wherever we went, out the chapel, down the steps,
along the walk, across the street around
the corner to the Globe, up the stairs, down
the stairs. I walked him like an older brother
who'd had a stroke, and he let me.

We talked so sweetly shuffling along.
He 70, me 61. He is absolutely fine
without anyone holding to him,

but it was so precious that muttering
and tottering around the September
Athens night. I recommend it.

Fall flat before the altar of poemgiving
and see if a friend is not tenderized
into some fresh foolishness
the two of you will never outlive.

This the animal you must imagine.
Part fox, part weasel, part
burrowing owl and dwarf.

You *are* this animal,
digging the tunnel of your secret.
You scratch and scratch,
and you have found the ore.

The vein is infinitely mineable,
inside the trance of work.

Now there is a soft-winged coo outside
above you. Your hands stop pawing
to listen: doves.

Harrison and 7th, Leadville, Colorado,
April 8, 2000, about 7 pm, crossing
from a coffeehouse to the Delaware Hotel,

rubberlegged and rubberarmed from driving
into the new height, ten thousand
two hundred feet above sea level,

I step out after two cars go by, not seeing
the third, small, white, blindspotted
mobile. My love Judith says
a faint *Don't go.*

I hold up. Faces in the car window upturn
to me like an unfolding cotton
tablecloth, so close,
not a foot.

This is where I could easily have ceased
to see out these coffee eyes, become
a mangled, dragged-along, inroaded,
gravel-clump, sog-sod bag
of *Don't go.*

And that topfloor sunset tall-window
turn-of-the-century room would not have held
our membranous circulations
so soon after.

My hand on your face's curve, I ask
for useful fear and letting go
whatever will not allow words to come.
I am so glad to be here.

There was a time when a man said poems
and friendship grew visible.

Whole evenings, phrases
came out of his mouth like breasts.
Language nourished with silence
as an infant opening for the nipple.

Naked words appear and enter the listeners.
It is not strange and dreamlike.
It feels natural and fully awake.

This might seem strange,
my standing reading words on paper.
I look up and speak and look down.

But I do not apologize. Now
is no less wonderful than then. We write
in a coffeehouse or parked alone in a car.
We print pages and revise on the porch
for months, years, tinkering.

I am climbing through a mist
rising off the Tennessee River in the 1940s,
down a bluff. No one knows I am.

On the shale ledges that slant and shelve
into the water are stone seashells,
fossils from the ocean that lived
when fish spoke cloud shoals
in the bright milk-mind of this child.

What does Yeats mean, *The heart grows old*?
The impulse toward romance
and sexual need gets less sharp?

I have a friend who has made himself
a saint of lust. Mac Intyre!

It is a quiet birdless Sabbath night
as I read Lowell, his final doubt
of the messiah. I admire his effort to say
what guidance we get in this clarifying
of unique light. Can we learn to listen?
To what and how and where?

Just before dawn, one candle in the cabin.
Can we follow what we are shown?
Is disobedience also the way
and patience an unnecessary suffering?

What does it mean to me, *The heart grows old*?
A few memories of my mother, dead now
thirty years. Her belief, when pressed,
was that the world began with Adam and Eve
in 4004 B.C., a Monday morning, January 1st.

When I went off to college and graded papers
in the religion department at the University
of North Carolina, we had a running argument
about that oriental document, Genesis B,
my mother an me, she on her couch-nest
flustered, I arrogant and cool in dad's chair.
Carbon dating fazed her less
than my dating.

   . . .

Mother had the innate joy of morning's
fresh matter, the shine of October
in the South. The war effort, the victory
garden and victory goat and rams and cows
running loose over the campus.
The magical cattle guard gate,
a xylophone under the Zephyr.

I used to go pretend grocery shopping
on my tricycle. Out from the cool moss walk
no sun ever hit, into the sun, pick up
some leaves and rocks, make a circle
inside the tower and come back
with the goods. Umm, good. What is this?
Fried chicken. What is this? Butter pecan
ice cream. Every day was an adventure
for my mother, and scary. Afraid of cars,
the bluff, afraid of hurting and falling,
mice and snakes and roaches. She never drank.
She woke pure emanation. I give myself
her mornings again, and listen to be led.

Last night I was shown in dream how to be
in front of a group without notes, or maybe
my fear of that. Anyway, no more arrant
New Critical chicanery. I bow to the mother
of morning and laughter and to the father
of smoke. My father's heart did
and did not grow old.

He was bored and bitter sometimes,
but the last six weeks of his life
he was more open than anyone
I have ever seen, filled with a big
no-worry, no holding-back love
for everyone he met. He could see

their souls there valiantly embodied,
singing their solo peeps
however they must.

Mother died in early May, he the 3rd
of July, bending to kiss the plume
of a lobby water fountain.

There is an ache in me when I say 1971
and 1942, a hollow *holler!*
That is how the heart grows old,
re-inhabiting the five-year-old
and thirty-four-year-old, empty
and fragile with working.

It is the end of some summer.
My parents are sitting out on the bluff
as the sun goes down, in those homemade
Adirondack chairs. Here comes the *Lake Queen*
excursion boat around the far bend under Lookout
with its watery tingle of dance music
and the second level which is all dancefloor,
and when they slide past this bluff, some
of them will come to the railing and wave.

I'll pull one of these heavy wooden chairs
over and sit with them. Hub and Bets.
What else might I do with this evening?
The reading and writing work
must wait on this love.

One thing we children would do was yell
across the river and Williams Island
and the river again straight into Elder Mountain.
Our voices came back small and perfected.
Just vowels were best, ooooooooooooooooooo,

but also short sentences like, *I can't hear you.*
or *Call me Raccoon,* which was its other name.

We played at letting the mountain say outloud
our given names, while it was always saying
with its deep green voice our most
secret selves to this day.

I cannot untangle the feeling of being exhausted
with the beauty of wind in the tops
of those trees and not here. Now here.

We slip through to another view,
yet we have not left. The heart grows
keen, quicker, and less here.

We were leaning against the hood
of my pewter Silverado, and I told her
how I came to buy it, which is not
the point here. I retold a fairytale
she had heard of but did not know,
and she told me about a person
she had taken three months off to help heal.

None of this is the reason I am working
pen and paper on the upstairs porch
after midnight. It is how
when we hugged goodbye, my hand went
innocently under her shirt to touch
the small of her warm silken back.

The feel of a woman's skin is my subject.
Along with the bridge of dying,
my granddaughter's skippy dance across,
water, and this elegant need to write.

Say we actually are as alert
as the black fly, wide as a quarter,
here in the woods, that I never see
until I pour out much-clotted sour milk
beside the cabin deck, and seconds later
they are thick in the clabber.

Same as when today the pipes are broken,
and I have to use the forest floor
for facilities. Before I have my pants
back up, they are on the stool.

I know a piano player who whirls himself
around saying *I have perfect stool.*
Are they everywhere, or do they come instantly
from somewhere, as we put out
the slimy hors d'oevres they adore:
like the motion of grace
to a sharp-felt prayer: Kosovo this Easter,
my son Benjamin's marriage breaking.

Black fly, rise and light on this rot
we have made. Massage it
with your myriad modified mouthparts back
to mulch and cool dark crumble
through the fingers.

Comes a sequence after sixty: set them
in the earth from the gate to the shed
you are beginning to use more.

Like the visit to Southwest Guilford
County High School in Greensboro, NC.
A kid raises his hand seventeen rows back,
What're we doing here?

It is 2:25 in the afternoon.
I have explained three times
that we are writing a quick half-page
about some time when we stole something,
or went against the rules some way.
Then we are going to experiment
with speaking those words with the cello.

He is quiet for a second. Shiiiiiiii. . . . .
He gets up and leaves by the side door.

A stone moment is then. You know you will not
be walking back in a high school, despite
how cold that might sound toward young people
and our obligations to them.

Still, there is the turn away
from those afternoon auditoriums.
Your part there is done. You may be back
in two years to that very room,
but for now it seems through.

*You do yo own petty theft and play it
on dee cello. I put yo cello in dee wello.*

* * *

The stone fits finely in the dug-out clay.
I tamp loose topsoil for edging
and sow the walk with tiny thyme.

In the 19th century in Georgia
there was a clever dog who found he could
secretly dig his way under the foundations
into the back of a meathouse.

The meat was hung to smoke too high
for his leap, but there were gourds
loaded with lard nearer his level.

The night he made his entry
was early in the century. The new residents
of the land were intruders themselves,
scared and cruel, so when they heard
the banging about, they did not investigate
until morning. The dog had gotten his head stuck
in a lard gourd. He could not see,
and he had almost smothered out there
in the helpless percussion of his night.

This ancient local color
allegorizes three of my troubling conditions:
blind desire, panic, and blackout drinking.

I have felt at times that I might be carrying
the living thread that connects
the sufi and zen currents,
also the vedantic and the high mountain shaman.

Then I get drunk, talk trash to a sweet saint
woman, fall out my top bunk, scare the children,
pee indoors, and I know the golden thread
I hold is pissant bad behavior
and not being present for the events of my life.

I am a bad dog with sex and alcohol.
I do not lead a pure life.

Then I remember the dog inside his lard
inside his gourd inside himself,
the dog that grows still and quiet.
I have somehow achieved these breathing holes.
I cannot see where I am going,
but I can breathe. Others have died
on nights like this. Maybe some human type
will find me and ungourd my head
and scrape this shit off
and groom my face with turpentine.

I fall on my knees to beg forgiveness
for meathouse-rude intoxication
and give all praise to the being
that lives and watches out, dog or not,
from the gummed-together eyes
of the lard gourd dog.

For those not of a monkish cast,
I'll explicate. The lard is the mind.
The gourd the container of that.
The meathouse, this temptatious world.
The dog is me. What gets quiet
behind the dog's eyes, survives and looks out,
has no name, except maybe *you.*

A child stood on his seat in a restaurant,
holding to the railing of the chairback
as though to address a courtroom.

Nobody knows what's going to happen next!

Then his turning-slide
back down to his food,
relieved and proud to say the truth,
as were we to hear it.

for Clinton and the Media

Bill, tell us what we all know: sex
is a holy joy, you at fifty,
she at twenty-three, in the erotic
cloud of Friday night, gentle genital touch,
lips on glans and lips on lips,
drinking the clear.

Henry Miller, Whitman, D. H. Lawrence, Galway
Kinnell, Edna St. Vincent Millay,
remember these saints of American honesty,
gone French, gone the Indian subcontinent's
tantric way, who ask us to say
our trance-truth, as we go into Faulkner's
no-time kamasutra of the late-night office.

It has been so long. I want this always.
You are so dear. You make me want to scream,
but I know we can't. When will we be brave
and live like Gabriel Garcia Marquez
in the glee of orgasmic caterwauling?

Instead, this *Scarlet Letter* Dimmesdale,
who stands on the scaffold pretending
to be forthright, with lipstick allegations
written all over the tube, when
he could be singing, I've got honey

*   *   *

in my heart and a barrel more besides.
Plus I am in the illustrious line
of fucking presidents, William Jefferson
Kennedy Roosevelt Johnson Clinton,
with here his saxophone kicking in

and a sweetie chorus doowopping
their obvious delight, and the big A
turns angelic crimson with gold threads
and green on a screen as tall
as Chimney Rock of thinnest neoprene.

A spring stars-just-out nine-thirty
when I was five, or four,
before school, that fear, before clothes,
I step from my bath, am held in the big towel,
then leap out to the front porch
and through the screen door along the curve
of boxwood, through the tower,
down its flight of three steps, next flight
next and next to the open ocean
of the quadrangle.

It does not seem like I am running,
rather more a thought sails into the night,
the idea of nakedness and Blakean joy,
with my parents and older brother
close in pursuit laughing
and finally reaching and snaring
the fleeing figure back to pajamas and bedroom,

but these fleet, insouciant feet
remember nothing of that.
They became evening air and a bit of sky
calmly taking another kind of bath,
with no telling how began
their adoration of moss in the cool brick walk.

How is it dogs know already
the big circling game they play with boys,
where the kid and the dog both get down
with forearms along the ground like sphinxes?

Then the boy runs at the dog,
and the dog takes off in a circle
that brings it back close enough
to be touched but not grabbed,
and changes tack to make a figure-eight
out the other side with the boy
in the hour-glass door.

The game needs a lot of space to do right,
a field, or a biggish backyard,
though I have seen it done on a steep hillside.

The look on the dog's face
is a tricky and barely embodiable joy.

There is an eruptive quality
on mother's side. One Thanksgiving
my cousin Tom Lamar was asked
to say grace, which was a joke since Tom
was way too religious for church
and so began, May the big pumpkin eat
the little pumpkin and all the buzzards
left of the river descend to the leafball
nest in the willow tree where sparrow lice
are waiting for the squirrel to return,
praise be.

Aunt Edith adds quietly, *Thankyee Jesus,*
and everyone sits down deadpan
until Sally's small one, Mary,
says *Can I open my eyes?*

When the way you propose to serve others
delights you, and the doing of it
brings in some, though very little, money;

when that way keeps you somewhat absorbed
in the so-called facts
of your life, and causes applause;

when you almost disappear inside it,
and if others seem nourished
in the outcome, shall we call that serving,
O fox, O hummingbird?

A guy with a shaved head, whom I have seen
often at the Globe, my go-for-a-few-beers
(or more) bar late at night, or more, caught me
peeing in the mop sink.

I had gone back and forth between
the two locked bathrooms
until some compromise was necessary.

We laughed, even though he was who
had to mop out the place after closing,
but what is so funny is, the night after
he found me tiptoeing up at the big sink,
he was mopping with the very mop,

while out of the local radio came
the live culprit, reading mystical poems
as though nothing of the sort.

for Bill Stafford

Between your four o'clock afternoon poetry
reading and dinner at the Chinese-Jewish
deli called Chow Goldberg, we stop here

at my house. You said you like to see
where poets live. Lots of uh-huh
and looking down the basement steps

and along the bookshelves. As we stood
in the kitchen having a glass of water,
you took the steel wool and Comet

and poured some of your water over
the top of my stove. Slowly the burner rims
grew chromy again. After supper

we went to a student dance concert.
You went justifiably to sleep,
and when you saw me mock-reproachfully

looking as you jogged awake, you did that
downturned mouth-shrug and little headback
motion I don't know where we all got.

My father did it. Stan Laurel, somebody,
taught it to us. You broke open
your tickled face with the wise Mongolian

. . .

eyes, and I whispered, "This would be
a nice place for a dance." You got solemn
and nodded sort of head-tilted,

then let the silent laughing loose
anyone could learn from to end up with.

Stacks of couchettes sliding sideways to
Toulouse. We two lying awake on top
bunks across from each other, writing

in journals with penlights, washed in
dream-drumming, absurdly happy,
splendidly silent. A love-ache guides

this school of narrow beds arcing like strands
of sound through a longhouse silver flute.
Your full eyes looking at me and now

in the dark asleep, little stations.
Between us before dawn, the face
of a thief intent, fingers probing

our baggage for wallets and cameras.
My eyes open into his. But now it must be
explained how we are on the way to meet

Jean-Louis Stahl, museum curator in Toulouse
who will get us into caves that are
normally forbidden. I love the Magdalenian.

Pretending then, this dark Portuguese
dock worker, cruel and quick and young,
arm gone to the bicep in our luggage,

to have mistaken this compartment for another,
says to me, "Jean-Louis?" From a dim
unraveling I reply, "Stahl?" Which can mean

. . .

in European languages, "a pretext for
clandestine activity" or "Stealing?"
It throws him off script. Hermes gives

a material glance, peek at the cooking,
catch you later, money quarrels in the morning.
The light and jagged laughs of our four

German masseuse suitemates understand
the incident in ways concealed from us.
Man and woman, reclining nudes

on continuous loan, slipping toward
a sanctuary of overlapping animals,
as the other we are runs thieving

through the train, misidentifying occupants,
footprints opposite and barely above
the gradually slowing, long-expectant clatter.

One year he let me touch him
under the iron steps.

One year to see his whole body
beneath the trilliums.

Now he has left a five-foot skin
across my stone threshold.

The great changing we give
comes as we slough winter
and glide like summer's low-roof
diamond-floor of invisible skin.

Sun leaving in the rearview mid-October.
Goodbye gorgeous air. Goodbye
shutdown ice cream store
with your sign saying only REAM. Goodbye,
leaf-traffic, goodbye Hairport 53,
goodbye boat storage sheds.

Goodbye serious concerns, goodbye prayer.
So long song, riding along with barely a sound.
Maybe not goodbye telepathy. Hello,
full telepathy.

Sunset has a little more to do.
You would not say it is night yet, not
the feel of that, though death is in the car,
sitting in the backseat, distracted
out the window, hat tilted on his head
like my father in the late afternoon
of the 1950s.

Goodbye four motorcycles on a trailer
being pulled. This feather-tinge
was the first image I ever wrote down,
the wake of some dark feather
that fell just now.

Goodbye, you pale rubbed glow.
Goodbye breathing out lightly the Mispeh
benediction, *While we are absent one
from the other*, Lord watch between.

. . .

Trees more black. Goodbye doubt, so dear to me
and not done yet, between two rows
of orange barrels narrowing.

Goodbye dog being patiently given water,
patiently lapping. Goodbye glass of water,
the slow huge dew forming everywhere.

Now in the frontseat with me,
sky its richest dark darkblue.

Goodbye, poetry. Big chunks of excitement
fly off in the nightair, no stars yet.

Goodbye holy softball halogen towers
of Bishop Park. Goodbye, God.
God be w'ye, God. The Christian fabric shop.
Goodbye corduroy, threads of the king.

Never goodbye laughter, never those I love.
The Sunday night driveway tunnels
through, key, message machine massaging.

Death intimately inside my forehead,
behind sight, lying on the couch in the dark,
with the door open and all the stuff
still out in the car. Goodbye home.

Prying the nameplate off the office door
that has been mine since this annex
was built, slipping a screwdriver
under the glued-on COLEMAN BARKS,

I make room for the linguistic
atlas-maker, drive home with the last
load of books, and weep.

Then I stop weeping. Country cemeteries
say he has gone to his rest,
this sweet afternoon nap, taking off
my glasses beside me on the bed,
ears afloat in phenomenal murmur.

Last night two dogs followed me
on my hour-walk. They picked up
on Springdale, McWhorter, Cherokee,
the way dogs will, walking ahead,

but staying with me no matter
the complications of the route,
young ones. All I said
was, *How you guys doing?*

I saw eternity the other night,
Like a great ring of pure and endless light,
All calm as it was bright.
—*Henry Vaughan*

There is an eternity around that looks out
and weeps from a place behind our eyes,
where we are grateful, from where
we recognize beauty, where lives

a dragon guarding unimaginable wealth,
and giving it away too, prodigal dragon,
a waterfalling darkness in the center
of the mountain, whatever *gold* means

to Renaissance alchemists, the fine refining
of self, the river's motion, waterlights
sliding along a cliff, a walk
in the evening, your arm lifted to a friend

a block away. God on the porch
a thunder and lightning June afternoon,
your jagged jot and scribble
on a piece of several-times-folded paper.

I love you, man. So we have these feet
to put boots on to investigate how it goes
about the building of Jerusalem,
this word-weary soul-world of footprint,

· · ·

footprint, waltz and samba. So go on.
This is ours to finish, or to leave
with a lot undone as you have. There is
some other thing you will no doubt

get good at. Someone turned one time
in a crowd of tourists leaving the Cathedral
of St. John the Divine in New York City
and said to me, a stranger, Don't forget

to turn out the lights. The week before
John died I was driving through the Fivepoints
intersection and had the thought
that John was about to change jobs.

I had meant to tease him about it but never
did, that definite premonition
of his death. A door opens in the side
of a cliff, looking through to a wide, empty

plain, beautifully bare. Behind the door
on the other side there is a cubbyhole
you could crawl into, but someone says
it has not worked. The winters are too severe

this high. One must not get cozy in a hideout
behind the death door, tempting niche
of grief. I may not be where I was when you last
saw me. I think these be true images,

the crawl-in cave near the wooden door
in the side of a grey cliff. They came in dream.
I long for scenes and notions of what lives
and lives through death. How friends continue.

. . .

Whatever makes the taste of laugh-look,
the talking so crystalline-passionate, though
unbreathable like the green air inside
an emerald. A young man is washing glass

double doors with a Windex pump-spray
and a rag. He has broken the middle finger
on his right hand. It is taped up,
grandly enlarged, and slightly curved,

so that despite his diligent demeanor
he is in magnificent, constant defiance.
We are glory-bound under a mosque-shaped
potato-cloud. Love those who can hear

your fear. Exuberance *is* beauty,
and clear reservations justly put are also
attractive. The road of excess leads
to the palace of wisdom, but not today.

Drive your cart and your plow over
the bones of the dead, and try sometime
to visit the tombs of Sufis singing *La,*
singing *La* illaha *il'Allah Huuuuuu.*

No major complaint, no minor insight.
The cry of the parrot is louder than the cry
of the turtle. Age is meaning and meaning
is killing us. Blake loves minute

particulars, but he does not get around
to mentioning many, as Whitman did,
spraying the pavement with sparkles off
a knife-grinder's emery wheel. A very

. . .

pregnant woman in Kinko's is carefully making
enlargement copies. Find your children
and sit down with them. Hot pies make
cold conversation. Baking takes precise

patience. Nakedness is the work of God.
Lust is the bounty of God. The laugh
of John Seawright is a tickling light in
the flower-throat of a summer late afternoon

glimmering out for a pointless drive
on the vast Athens bypass. So open the five
inlets of soul as lightning bugs come forth
at 17 to 9. What do they do all day?

They down there in the dirty with they lights
off getting work done like the rest of us.
Nightimes's for cruising. You know,
they think they have found what it is allows

a lightning bug to cut himself on and off.
Nitric oxide, the same chemical that
controls heart rate and memory in humans.
Some cell in a lightning bug combines

with air to make nitric oxide, which scientists
call NO. At a spontaneous signal from
the lightning bug's brain—consider that—
the NO gets released. Adjacent cells

shut down. This gives off a pulse of oxygen
which triggers an enzyme that turns on
the light, all in a millisecond says Barry
Trimmer, biologist at Tufts. Sara Lewis,

.   .   .

fellow firefly expert, says there are 200
different species with 200 different signaling
sequences. Lightning bugs live for two years
as larvae in the soil. Then only two weeks

as adults in their courtship phase. Life
is intense and short. *Glow, little glowworm.*
It is the males who send sequences. Females
answer, one wink. But this could change

next week when the current lightning will have
panned away. Mark Twain said the adequate
word is to the right word as a lightning bug
is to lightning. He is right, but he had not

heard a thing about the big NO with its release
to YES, as the folds of time and place circle
like a pony at the end of a Coriolis rope
riding the horizon in layers of iridescent

intelligence. There is surely more to this
flint-rant, pool-umbrella love for thunderstorms.
Shenanigan chiaroscuro, mover-along, a man
sits on his bed with his bare feet on the floor,

leaning back all the way flat, arms out foot
to head, one palm east, the other west.
This is such a comfortable posture to listen
to the measures kindling, others draining

through gravel. And after that your feet make
no print, nor scatter any pigeon, nor dig
one heel for purchase, nor slide nor dance,
and I wait for how to say the blank forehead,

.   .   .

a peeled stick, the hesitant, doldrums soul,
a pine cone with rolled mud for legs.
The helpless terror, the flung note. Two crows
walk in smooth sand making a single sentence,

that is also conversation, with insect-peck
punctuation. Now one lifts, then the other,
into open air again, and a man is quickly
climbing the theatre balcony stairs.

John Seawright's Epitaph
Love brought me this far by the hand, then
just kept standing there, not letting go.

FROM *CLUB: GRANDDAUGHTER POEMS* (2001)

If I were dying, or if I were convinced
I were dying soon, say within a year, if
I were told so by doctors, I would write
a bunch of poems out of my nervousness
and my love for being here. They would be
what I saw on walks and times I would spend
on the phone with my granddaughter remembering
when we went to the Shrine Circus, and Julio
tried the triple and missed, and there was no
finale. They just announced—when we all
expected there to be something else, at least
a parade of clowns and elephants and jungle-ladies
riding by—"Thank you for coming, folks. Let's
hear it for the Shrine Circus!" But we have more
than memories. We have polaroids. Briny took
them, of brightly lit jugglers and the little girl
acrobat. She'd look through the camera hole
and then look up and snap it, but when she looked
up, the camera would tilt a little down, so
we have a number of photographs of circus dirt
with a part of a spotlight circle at the top.

Some Monday nights we meet after supper, no
moms or dads allowed, I'm grandfathered in.
The only organization I'm part of—no nation,
no religion, no academic business anymore.
We do science experiments like walking around
the block to check on Hale-Bopp. She wears
special shoes, genie silk numbers that turn up
at the toe. She invents people that live in houses
we pass. Teacher Jane with lights on her arbor.
She has funny hair. Green. Uh-oh, here comes
a broken Milk of Magnesia bottle. It's the blue
swamp. I'll carry you across. One night we met
at the new house they'll soon be moving to. She
takes me upstairs to show which room will be hers,
empty except for a metal office desk. Students
have been renting the house. She opens a side
drawer and tears off a piece from an adding machine
roll. This is your *permanent* ticket to club. I
never had a permanent ticket before. I put it in
my pocket and later while we're drawing pictures
notice that it has monkishly careful writing on it.
Tiny calligraphy, amazingly, of the first three
and a half poems from Rumi's *Birdsong*. Somebody
copied out the entire book on that role. I do not
pretend to know what's going on, but I was there
re-membered into a body, a flock, when Briny
reached in like a little bird and handed me
my permanently torn ticket stub to club.

She is worried about Wietien, a student new this week,
who knows no English. Three first graders
have been assigned as helpers, Briny for reading,
someone for lunch, Landon for recess.
They are learning colors. Briny points to a swatch.

Can you say *pink*? *Canyousaypink*, he says back
perfectly, which is pretty funny. During recess
Landon plays with the boys, and Wietien stands
to one side in one place for the half-hour. The girls
do jump-rope, only girls there. What can she *do*

about Landon's not helping Wietien? If I were this
concerned for some new person, or you, who looks
leftout, the cities would glow inside their murk.
Wietien is the best in class at math, better than
anybody, because numbers are a universal language,

she mimics her teacher, numbers and music. How about
kickball and dodgeball, or just plain throwing back
and forth? The play of old rivers through Alps Road
Elementary is the music of this morning, among
the mountains of these children, so fragile and carefully met.

Briny and I put on a show for an audience
of one, her father, my son Benjamin.

She writes out the program: her part a play
called, "A Cabin Compared to the Beach,"

mine, "A Poem on Daydreaming, read by Coleman
Barks." Her play has many characters, Max,

Susanna, Nicole, a King and a Queen, and some
others I forget. There is a lot of sleeping

and waking up and several set changes. It
is a marvel of rich-and-poor, a golden

tablecloth, and a final choosing of ocean
over remote cabin. I could not possibly

recreate it. I looked in several anthologies
for something spunky enough to be on the same

bill; found only Emily Dickinson. Only her,
out of *Seven Centuries of English Poetry.*

"To make a prairie it takes a clover and one bee.
One clover and a bee, and reverie. The reverie

alone will do, if bees are few." Then came
our freeform bee-witchery: train whistle

out the window. To make a train it takes a whistle
and some track. The whistle alone will do,

.   .   .

if track is too expensive. To make a mountain
range it takes some snow and a funny hat,

The funny hat alone will do, if snows be few.
To make a car it takes a wrench and lots

of iron. The wrench alone will do, if you
can't find iron. To make a little girl

it takes a trinket and some silver. The
trinket alone will do. To make a reverie

it takes a prairie and one girl. The girl
alone will do, if the prairie is on fire.

Briny playing with two friends, boys around
her age, decides they should pair up in all

possible combinations, the two boys, one boy
and her, the other and her: the idea is

the two should talk about the one, say anything,
no matter how mean or gushy, each pair

out of earshot of the single. But she accidentally
hears them say something about her and gets

her feelings hurt. She is crying beside me
on the front steps. What did they say?

That I was too young, that I should grow up.
I kiss the top of her head. *I feel like such a jerk,*

she says and gets up in the bravery of her stride
with a new proposal: *now let's stand together*

and say all the things we've said about each other
to each other. A Shakespearean grandeur enters.

Let the door be locked. They say and drink
the poisons they've been secretly tipping

their tongues in. Look: this is the way: to either
live in the spirit that watches our drama,

laughs at, and is compassionate toward,
the jealousies and woundedness and greed

. . .

and fearful panic and fierce paradings our masks
memorize the lines for, or die trying.

Shakespeare mostly strewed his final acts
with corpses before Prospero. The blue jewel box

of my Virgil opens to tell me *pro-spero*, to hope
forward into, favored one, to read in this

experimental life the auspices. Behold, I show you
three brave jerks, who will give it a try,

to speak and be the truth. My sister once said
when I was getting willfully drunk and mean

and jealous, *What happens to your Rumi self?*
Fifteen years later I hear her sentence

in the giant hollow of an empty amphora
buried in the earth to its lip, where Plato

and Socrates talk, where Rumi and Shams sit
in *sohbet*, where my sister Betsy and her morning

voice, where Bill Stafford and his. There is
another talking, a fermentative way

that Briny is trying to break through to
with her various gamey Gurdjieffian ploys.

When the adults are talking house renovation,
pregnancy and strange automotive encounters,

she and her buds do new work for humanity
in the front room. Time will put us all in that

* * *

audience, but we need not wait. We are now
the discourse with dreams and granddaughters

and the next walker coming toward us
on the street. I do not want to ever finish this

poem. We are who with courage we might
become. Or to sound less triumphal and leave

a loose edge to come back to: we sing with friends
in an underground room as a lowriding rap

beat thumps by in the streetlight above.

We are riding out in the green Dodge, '72
homemade convertible, to fly a bought boxkite,

which we do one windy day a year, past
the Presbyterian church. Do you go there?

I sing in the chorus sometimes. Mom says
she doesn't feel the need for church. Well,

it's all church, don't you think? This is church.
She smiles, full assent. Yes. Nothing

more needs be. It is so windy, a steady
thirty miles an hour that afternoon, it takes the kite

and all our stinging-handed stringery, grabs
the pink plastic holder from our grip, tumbling

across the field to hook on barbed wire, break
and let the kite sink beneath the treeline

toward town, the whole exhilarating ceremony
not more than a minute and a half. We then

walk around the field eating red clover,
find a shed with pressed tin ceiling panels

nailed to the inside walls, and not finding
the lake, we end on our backs

watching cloud-clover rush and reshape.

We play dumb chess, which is each
trying to get in checkmate first,

two bumbling buddy kings out on
the heath in high good health, see,

because you can't move into check,
a kind of foolish minuet. Once

the whole bunch moved off the board
to the pattern on the rug, and they

could talk when you held them close
to your mouth. The white were

Californians, the black were India
Indians. The rooks were angry

workmen plotting mischief for the
children, herding the knob-headed

little dopers through the garden.
Here come the mothers to save us.

In the glory of the gloaming-green soccer
field her team, the Gladiators, is losing

ten to zip. She never loses interest in
the roughhouse one-on-one that comes

every half a minute. She sticks her leg
in danger and comes out the other side running.

Later a clump of opponents on the street is chant-
ing, WE WON, WE WON, WE . . . She stands up

on the convertible seat holding to the wind-
shield. WE LOST, WE LOST BIGTIME, TEN TO

NOTHING, WE LOST, WE LOST. Fist pumping
air. The other team quiet, abashed, chastened.

Good losers don't laugh last; they laugh
continuously, all the way home so glad.

She explains tackle football. You
pass the ball between your legs, you
go hurt somebody, then you start over.

You pass the ball between your legs,
you go hurt somebody, then you start
over. When everybody is hurt, the game

ends, because the people in the stands
don't want to get hurt, they just like
to see others. Two-hand touch is better.

She asked me did I have poems for
children. They were doing poetry.

And would I write one that had her
name in it. I don't think I do

have any poems second graders would
listen to. Mine are too old or not

lively enough or they might mention
something they are not supposed to

hear about, like the girl Claudia,
ten, watching television, who said

*Mom, I am not old enough to watch
this.* But now maybe this could

turn into something they might like
because I am remembering Claudia's

younger brother Rob went to a museum
and saw Lucy, the name scientists

have for the early almost human ape
woman they found and reconstructed

how she looked millions of years ago.
She is hairy and naked and stooped over

with her hairy breasts hanging down
and she is carrying a bone for a tool,

*   *   *

and she is about fifty feet high
on the museum wall and Rob sees her

and can't stop looking and he keeps
saying as they're walking around other

places, *I can't stop thinking about*
Lucy the ape woman. Mom, I can't

Get her out of my mind. Then he's quiet
for a long time, and then he says,

I bet she was pretty for her time.
Now two Rob stories that cannot be

read to second graders. Rob tells
his mother about a song other children

sing on the school bus. It has
the f-word in it. I beep it. *Every time*

it comes up I beep it. Do you know
what it means? *Yeah, sex.* Some older

boys must have taught it to them. He is
quiet. Don't you think they must have?

OK, OK. I wrote that song. But I beep
the f-word when I hear it. Rob's

a songwriter and a film critic. Once they
were in a movie lobby in the popcorn

line. Rob was fiddling with himself in
the pants area. Honey, do you need to

* * *

go to the bathroom? *No. I'm just
getting my penis ready for the movie.*

The teenage couples behind them collapse
with laughter for maybe the most telling

cinematic observation I have ever heard.

FROM *GOURD SEED* (1993)

I love the microphone breath-flutter,
the famousness of words, that keeps me up late
and remote from a cigar-sweet closet
under the stairs where an old man
reads his Bible and hears the encores
and turns out the overhead to nap,
with applause so softened and made
whole by the basement walls.

Deep Sleep is his name, and just by not dying,
he refreshes, as dawns have my life so rarely,
though now less rarely. More often,
he talks and walks me through the scripture
of aching light, the way he's hoped he could.

Before I get in,
the aluminum canoe floats flat on the shine
of water. Then I ruin its poise.
Middle of the first shoal, though, I'm out,
stumbling through the ankle-breaking rocks.
Canoe free-floating downstream, without decision
or paddle. I lunge and bruise across the shallows
to get a forefinger in the rope eye on the stern.

June afternoon light. June afternoon water.

I know there's a life being led in lightness,
out of my reach and discipline.
I keep trying to climb in its words,
and so unbalance us both.
The teacher's example is everywhere open,
like a boat never tied up, no one in it,
that drifts day and night, metallic dragonfly
above the sunken log.

These flowers outlast
the houses they delight
to walk out from in thin spring dresses
to where relatives used to live, when they were new lovers,
with now cedar trees growing through the bedsprings
by the three grey stone steps that lead nowhere.

The brain-bulbs twin and quadruple
in the translucent ground.

And whatever we say or do is a new clove
on the cluster we're with,
that helps the cup-shapes come up,

that have no use I know of,
except to hold your cheek close
and let someone see if it reflects,
which tells if you love
buttermilk or not.

Or maybe that was just the ending
our family had for the ritual.
I have never liked buttermilk,
though I've not tried it for forty years.

I shall taste again, I promise
into these frilly, old-fashioned telephones
that stand here without their ear-pieces,

what my father never understood
why nobody else but him enjoyed,
the bitter breast,
that left a froth of surf-lines
in his ordinary glass.

Down off a steep-hanging Darjeeling
mountainside my feet fumble
a stairstep path through bare, tin
shacks. Bare, outside.
What we enter is a marriage,
shining with dark wood and candles
and silver bowls of springwater
and fresh tanka paintings, fierce blue,
life-changing males, and the green woman.

Each bell has gender. I tell my visitors
to close their eyes, now clear
on the other side of this elaborate planet,
and lightly waggle to let them guess.
Sweet gossip.
                    One of the beautiful early-
Twenties daughters has her brother
tell my friend she likes me.
                              O talk more,
metallurgy. How resonating absorbs
and gives back a wave-weaving
from a center as it receives
the other.
                    I want to love you
in that precarious town pitched
on the spine of a Himalayan ridge.

I want an inwardness
that is nothing familiar,
a rosy, tea-colored sky
moving like shelter,
in balance.

Give it to the next fellow.
Not the ten dollars, the help. No mistaking
what he meant or saw the afternoon as,
a fine chance. The 1965 tractor started up,
though one of its brakes kept sticking, amusing him.
I'd gotten as far as I could trying to find a new walk,
to a gate bar across the road and backed back and onto
soft shoulder, slid helplessly into the ditch, hopeless
to maneuver out of. Walked to the nearest house.
He came to the door still chewing his lunch,
then went toward the barn, I making polite apology.
You're heading for that tractor, aren't you?
If it won't start, we'll get a horse.
The man who wants no credit, or even to shake hands,
too busy with what needs doing, holds his arms
close in and sidles by me in the barn
like I'm a ticklish passage, me holding out my money.
Give it to the next fellow.

There is a huge holly tree next to where I glided to a stop,
a solid thigh-trunk white-splotched
and stretching deep under the dishwater.
Beauty, but not such as this man is,
beyond any tree.

Flying done in sleep woodenly with arms,
slow-stumble-flight, making a moment
disproportionate, ten feet over the creek,
this presence I want to run after, but don't,
seen now and once before.

Up the hill planting trees,
one dogwood, two flowering peach,
kneeling in the cool Easter dirt,
on the last one, devotional and vain,
why turn and look,
I don't know, but here's the biggest bird
I've ever seen, huge, bluish-grey,
stretching between hemlock and laurel,
moving slow against the creekwind,
legs and body hanging almost straight down.

Wait, says this presence I'd forgotten could exist,
*wait. Don't stay up late
imagining, neither awake not asleep.
Be exhausted,* lifting
off the balcony in a backdive.

Jim Kilgo says what I saw was a Great Blue, a heron,
not a crane, "though people call it a crane."

The first crane I saw was when I was seven
with Lucian by the lake, the black man
who worked at the barn and lived there
above the tack room, he with his shotgun at sunset.
Two glowing cranes
flying high and west, no struggle or wobbling
at that height. Maybe he didn't think
shotgun pellets could reach that far. Idle,

curious aiming. Blam. A long moment.
The following crane folded and dove
like a starving pelican and sank so
when Lucian rowed out there was nothing.

That was summer 1945.
Two atom bombs. Nobody knew
what they were. Now with cranes
so rare, I'd push the gun
off toward empty air,
if I were quick enough.
I want to purify myself with constant love,

till the vision of a six-foot beanpole crane
stretched over the creek
be just a sight I have at five-fifteen, March 23rd,

with praise for being awake, for sleep,
for memories from both coming clear,
as happens,
when I'm not afraid of being, being
the gooney, flying bird's head with long spoonbody,
or the other I see in the carwindow's reflection
with vague eyes full of fear
It's a look encouraged here,
not likely to be shot,
unless it let go and rise
from the wading pool
in a new knowing.

Coley and I once talked to a screech owl
that flew in and down the stairwell,
and lit, swear to God, on the top rim
of Coley's big picture he drew of an owl.
When I held up Coley's left crutch,
(a broken leg bike-jumping off a ramp)

the owl stepped on to the end
and glared fire riding the crutch
to the door. Fear and rage distilled,
clamped in place in that small body.

Owl turns to the night behind him, turns back
to us standing on the doorstill, then the weight
on the end of the crutch leaves,
four wingbeats and a long slide
through trees. That's what it's like
to be healed.
These birds are pictures of our being alone,
at large: light flight,
then back to a fearful perch.

We are such fluttering monsters
moving within several shapes, till some appearance
surprises: A new love
puts her head to my chest
and listens.
Later a call
from that direction, Yhhhhhhhuuuuuuuuu

Fear.

Years inside a sleep, the woods
melt to an edge of trees, speech
trails off in a field, my child
forgets what he wants.

You reappear and stand beside a house.
You ask to trade places.

I shall be the written words and you walk out
among this other.

You whisper into me, *You have made love to just about everyone
there is. Now it will be me doing that.*

I understand, I become these long writings.

I believe in things that were strange before:
the tangle of figures in Malaysian art, something waiting
inside the haloed heads of Flemish paintings. NO gold
around his baldness at all, the patron kneels
with his hat in front of him on the ground.

The current where it dips around a rock
has strands of light inside it.

The fields are covered with forest again.
My dreams come back more clearly.

That we recognize each other
is the finest act there is,
naked and nervous in these small white diagnosis rooms.

* * *

This is the true condition of middle age.

We pick our way through the brush, lifting branches
with whole cities lightly attached, that falling,
are not cities at all.

They may not go back to their marriages.
Tonight they're frying
slices of green tomato in the dorm room.
They don't know what's going to happen.
I'm just passing through this six-week
summer program for honors students,
two days and I'm gone. These two
new lovers are teachers for the whole
month and a half, with two weeks to go.

They are finicky about the heat on the electric frying pan.
She slices the green tomato toward her with the paring knife.
He does the flipflop of the flouring.
I put a thick layer of mayonnaise on the whole wheat
and arrange the lettuce leaves,
happy enough not to have love problems.
I love them both.

Let green tomatoes stand for innocence.
The frying pan for how much they want this love they have
now, longer. Though everything stands for that,
to them. Then who am I over here
with my knife in the mayo,
hungry as anybody else? No woman
fixes supper with me
regularly. May be
I should worry more about that
than I do. She is here, I tell myself,
but unseen, unmet, as yet.

I'm no priestly bachelor, for God's sake.
Though I do honor the calm, sweet light
around these two, I don't long to be
in love again, their kind, but I do
long for love to fill me. I can't explain

what kind. I help them fix and eat
their strange green sandwiches
and feel like I can wait
less restlessly now
that I have been here with them,
doing this.

We get it in our heads
to inspect the undersides of each
waist-high Queen Anne's lace,
to find the black bug always at home
in his apartment of green scaffolding.

I don't understand why we want each other so much.
Some of my wanting is curiosity.
Each time, here's someone living inside.
I want you. I want you.
What are we saying.

Eventually we can eat the flower of our need,
bug and all,
and we're just out walking nowhere,
with no schemes.

She whimpers in her sleep,
when I move in half-sleep, quarter.
She makes with me, for me, small, consoling, fearful
sounds, *urrhhh, unnnnrrhh,* as a mother cat
talks to blind kittens, comforting and warning,
afraid they're about to get up and leave.

We go on tossing, talking to each other,
not conscious. I see it
in the robes and draperies,
folds of sheets and covers so in need
and moving, white edges of waves,
bedless, houseless bedclothes
with naked lovers, swaying
exhaustion, ocean kelp.

And the same robes and draping
frame mystical paintings, clothing
scenes of God's presence—Gethesemane,
twelve-year-old Jesus with the elders, Jerome
in the wilderness, da Vinci and Dali,
Winged Victory, and damsels from Rubens, tangled
in the same cloth, definite folding
edge, and changing.

Answer something to her grieving desire,
falling back into comfort and no-comfort.

We're waiting till it's over,
this strange energy-ocean.

* * *

It is a chief mystery to me
how we last as long as we do,
seventy, eighty years.

There must be some tender, possible, other-place,
composed of land, a tree, shade,
a bench with an old man talking about death,
maybe even the moment of death,
both of us taking sips of tea
the color of air with the sun going down.

Is this an old nostalgia, to sit
with whoever we call philosopher, father, him
and his quizzical questions: Whether things are different
or the same, whether I believe the thing I deny,
what we both can know. I want to hear
his tone in this conversation.

Instead, we're walking through an open basement,
nothing left but brick piers. Between them,
mounds of thick shards of glass, jade,
ruby, bright orange-yellow. We call it
the glass factory, my brother and I.
It looks like an abandoned industry. Who knows.

Sacred and unexplained, dangerous to the fingers,
It is not a place I can believe the image
of bedcovers and luminous paintings
all being the same. That does not seem true now,
even such a short time afterward,

though the wanting to sit on a bench
and talk calm and honest
with an old man
remains.

Some days it seems like a spontaneous play.
All I have to do is nod and laugh and watch
what comes next, with great interest.
The waitress approaching for a coffee refill,
"Now you're going to learn what

                    fear is."

And here's John Hillenbrand, trying to convince me
to go fishing with him, describing a bream
that's too big to hold in one hand to get the hook
out. "You have to press it to your shirt
to keep it still, working

               the barb loose,
that's a *titty-bream*." With us, listening,
is Lisa, of the most beautiful breasts I've seen,
ever. They curve like wide banana boas. They are
wise. The adrenalin is noticeably revving
in our fish stories. In the parking

                  lot later,

she says the stars are more out, out
in the country where she lives. One night
they found Saturn accidentally. *The rings
were clear, and two of the moons.* "Please call,
if you get that in your lens again,

                  Lisa."

I've always wanted to look deeply into a glass
tunnel and see Saturn at the far end.
But I wait too well for the near as well
as the far. I haven't had the presence
to say, "I would love to undress you.

                  Let's go

• • •

to the starlit country." Naaoooooow. Soul,
dear face and breasts of Lisa, whatever I want so
much, the carwind late-at-night, no one on the road,
light in the eyes and on the water, secret light
inside a telescope, my passions,
                              don't be afraid.

Sleek and near, I lift you and whisper
in your mouth how I love the deep coldness
that made you and holds you with Saturn,
warm against cool, our favorite nakedness,
feeling the live bream
                    against my chest.

Green, the shape of a man,
with the insides of a woman.

They swim and dive around each other
in the boiling water, like porpoises.

O, to put the whole pod
of okra in the mouth.

Tomatoes, it is time to taste
ourselves, in these wet, red rooms,
the rooms of our mouths,
where lives the sigh
of language.

Corn, the tassels pull apart,
ears and silk, ears and silk and teeth.

Cantaloupe, a globe in tight webbing,
crisscross imprint. The onion underground,
in crumbs of dirt and old fabric.
Heat waves take form. Without panic or fear,
the air becomes visible.

Cucumbers, turning and sinking in the vinegar bowl.
I hold a head of cauliflower in my hand.

It's the head of someone whose name escapes,
which is not so strange. There are many names
for the ones we love, and wonderful to say:

. . .

Broccoli, Lettuce, Cabbage,
String Beans, Snow Peas, Pear,
Watermelon, Pomegranate, Plum.

Let us eat the solid forms of sunlight,
and walk around after supper
in the gold time,
loving each other and talking vegetables.

This woman I am with
is having her palm read
by my friend. I am not allowed
near. I go off up the hill to gather
kindling in the apple basket. Cracking small limbs
from the brush, I see them down on the deck,
laughing, faces close, hands
mending together.

Here with the sticks,
I find something, a numeral,
a wooden number one, streaked and flaky red,
with a rusted chain attached. I carry it
back with the full basket, hang it
over the fireplace, and wait
for praise.

Forty-five and sour with jealousy,
I wish this would pass,
and I would give up,
like these dry water-throats,
to being just a friendly,
apple-munching fire.

The flame in the fireplace is the hair
of this room, of our being,
the going and staying waterfall
I light to watch fall up.

There is no sharp division between flame
and its light. Fire loosens
in the cells of the log a closed hotel
of rooms, loosens wood like string,
unties water, psssssswwwwwwwww,
opens the dead xylum.

It runs along beside me, it walks, it runs,
it has strong feelings about everything.

And no edge defining it
from its light.

A slight pressure of spring air.
We hold our breaths together
to stop your hiccups.

Listen to the machines, the sound of my salary:
coffee-maker, washing machine, stove-eye
boiling, and here the car comes back.

I'll tell you, since you cannot see inside here,
reader, we are fixing supper,
we're drinking red wine on the stoop,
and eating corn on the cob
as it gets done.

I imagine the demons will find us again,
as they did last night.
Forgive me if you can. Today,
I am the blind man
sticking his head out the window.

A moral question for the institution: How *long*
to keep coming out by this pond in Oconee County,
hoping the dog will show up, the dog
my son lost track of here unbelievably,
she's such a whiny crybaby wanting total
attention and constant contact, and what
he was doing anyway with his friend Jim and Jim's dog
on Jim's father, Rufus' many hundreds of acres, remains
mostly unanswered. This is my fifth time out twenty miles,
walking this kudzu-engulfed-and-lizarded road
to hear App bark just once. All the way in to the slime pond
with the rotten dock, up through pines past
a deer stand to a scrawny orchard
with my whistling and calling, baffled
that a runt-of-the-litter, five-year-old, spayed collie
could be lost in this tangle, or ever leave the safety
of the road for any reason. I try to grieve
for my dead dog, and my cold, quick son,
who seems so little concerned, and uncatchable
in his escape cars. I have not cried yet
over the dog, gone four nights, probably
lying down eaten up with ticks and mosquitoes and hornets,
or shot by someone for a fox, or maybe alive,
decided to go wild, unlikeliest
chance. This long.
Tonight's the last after-supper run.
Then I'll put ads in the papers, and it's up to how
it is to be. In my mind now she seems a little, loose,
leathery pod, like those hanging on a bush
outside my cabin, and I'm not there so I can't check
whether this one's rotten inside, or broken open
with whatever it is free and flying around with

orange circles on its lavender wings,
close to my face.

Second stanza.
The girl down the street whom I've called
"sentimental doglady" goes out, two and a half weeks after,
knocks on every door of a housing development,
locates word of a thick, tick-crusted
something, wandering the area. She stays and waits
with her husband, and there's the dog!
By God, I change my tune about crying and giving up hope.

We are driving back from *Hamlet* at the Anniston,
Alabama, Shakespeare Theatre, going to a cabin
on Weiss Lake near the Georgia line. It's after twelve.
A green Camaro comes past the other way and does
a sliding one-eighty turnaround in a dirt road
intersection. I see it in the rearview
and speed up, suspecting some playful, country
viciousness, the kids excited like it's a movie.

The Camaro stays inches off my back bumper, no matter
I'm going eighty-five or fifteen. He does not leave.
I make a big loop-circle through a closed service station,
he's there all the way. He even pulls off the road and stops
with me, three inches behind. It is the strangeness
of not being able to see his eyes to gauge
how demented. This is not a movie.
It is such a shadow-whitened full moon night,
he cuts his lights to disappear for a second, then
reappear as a dark bulk speeding in place.
He *does not* pull in the driveway.

The following afternoon in the parking lot
at Desoto Falls, here's the Camaro with a guy leaning
on the front fender. *Would you like a beer?* Sure.
He goes back to open the trunk to fetch it,
I guess, from a cooler. "No thanks, that's
all right." I can't see walking over and him handing
me a beer, if that's what it was to be.

Whoever finally catches up with me and says pay
for all incompletely-lived, held-back-on
moments will be some innocent stockcar fan
with no idea what he'll do next.

. . .

I love to see it and talk about it, Shakespeare's truth,
but I have never said Hamlet's lines that change him,
those with the practice tip off the sword.

Any number of vague, driven moments might be out looking
for me now, some one of my random craziness
I could let stand for comeuppance. Shakespeare
has ways to open the curtains wider, out-loud attitudes
toward having run out of choices in front of a bunch
of people. I don't know what to say next till I am
what I know now, and that not constantly enough,
so my talking's about half-believable.

It's clinically wrong, but this begins with a drink,
alone, back from the emergency room, cortisone
in each hip, welts heating up in clusters
on right arm, chest, back, inside right thigh, left
shoulder, and between the eyelid and eyebrow,
twenty-one stings. I'm not sure
yellow jacket or hornet. Doctor says it doesn't matter,
both hymenoptera, *Little mean bastards,*
they go for the eyes.

A wonder of innocent membranous wings again
after six years, come to me not wandering, but in
my own remote meadow-yard, swingblading
what I take to be my duty of tall weeds. Now
days of itchy skinconsciousness, thankful
to be anywhere, burning to scratch blood. They smell me
with my venomous sensitivity, me especially.

I have heard what some objective someone said: *Coleman*
is riddled with fears. Well that may be,
and the problem then: to boil what mixture I have
into soup, a glad courage to be sipped as I walk
back without a shirt to retrieve the swingblade
where it fell, skin so awake to air
and any slight furry hair of bee that lights,
forerunner, pre-bee of swarm-to-come
that cannot be fended off, the thought of which
musn't. Last night this dream. A woman
lines up juice glasses, drinks for me, clear liquid.
In the bottom of each, under ice cubes, is a live,
moving-its-legs, bee. I'm expected to drink
the stingers down. I'm hesitating.

●　●　●

I didn't see what I hit in the grass that caused this.
Often it's clearer. I have known when I was swinging
into a hive-nest and gone on slow-motion
with a long swing. Make-happen and let-happen
and other happens out of nowhere. I cannot untangle
the green wire, but I know the feel of that sound
around my head. Swollen, blackening, and finally
patient, it gives me new eyes to see the lovely
obstructions, the bamboo scaffolding.

The air only seemed to be thickening into knots
that kill. I didn't foreknow these beestings.
I had the dream, but no clarity, the way now
I have angry bee-acid in me swelling
to circulate. Look at this line of drinks,
a future of juice glasses, each with a scarab
waking more and more in the melting
and the hesitation.

These are fearful gifts that I accept,
and cautiously hold to the light, and swallow,
biestings, the old word for the first milk,
which is clear, from the mother's breast.

Now you'll be crazy over bees, says Benjamin, long distance,
among my other fears of motorcycles, power tools, snakes
on low-hanging branches, and I summon them all
to let them hum around my head, one at a time.
I don't need another black hood of buzzing.
More than three, I hit the water quick,
and you can laugh if you want to.
I choose to watch my daylight panic as a rock does,
secretly covered-uncovered in the stream.

An old drunk, probably about the age I am now,
broke in our house before I was born, broke in
my brother Herb's room. Herb was small and sick
with a fever and not at all frightened
by the stranger standing there.
                              "Would you like
some orange juice?" He held out the glass of it
he had on the bedside table. Then Dad appeared
with a baseball bat and led the man off, whose
name escapes. No one was hit, or prosecuted.

All that resulted from that bemuddled night was
that twisted-iron bars as though for a castle
were fastened on all our bedroom windows,
and I grew up looking out through those bars
at the river, and climbing on them.

I know more now of the blank confusion he felt,
the drunk, and I've done unconscious things too
that have had consequences like the way he affected
my view of the outside for years, who was not even
born then, and who has just as blind a notion
of what bad or good could come of some wandering,
dumb thought to go and do I don't quite know
what.
          Could I offer you some orange juice?

My forty-nine entries
to the Name the Call Letters Contest
won me seventeen albums, but not the movie camera.

Under various names—Xenia Zed, Mrs. Jarvis Helms,
Lothar Tresp, Matthew Barrick—
through two contest weeks, carrying a pack
of blank postcards, mailing them
from different bars around Athens: The Chameleon,
The Frogpond Lounge, The Last Resort,
Friends, finding anagrams
in drunktalk, winsome,
raunchy, four-letter conundrums:

WIND REALLY FONDLES COWS
WENCHES ROAR FOR CHASTITY
WRITING RARELY FEELS COMFORTABLE
WHAT REACHES FROM CHINA

Thomas Wolfe made lists
of what he had to eat, who he slept with,
towns and cities, menus, casual sex.
The *I Ching* says there's nothing wrong
with casual sex. A girl I met in a bar
in Norfolk threw the coins to ask.

WHICH ROOM'S FOR CHEATING
WHO RUNS FOR CHEESE
WIMPS RUN FOR CONGRESS
WEAR RATTY FUR COATS
WITH REVERENCE FOR CUCUMBERS
WE'RE RUNTS FROM CAMILLA

. . .

You see people walking by the ocean picking up shells
and shark's teeth to put in a dish on top
of the counter in the kitchen.

WIDE RUNGS FEEL CONFUSED
WHIPPING RUINS FAT CHILDREN
WALLY'S RICH FINGER CREAM
WILD RHINOS FLATTEN CABBAGES
WHARF RATS FORGET CHRISTMAS

There is no end to that either, the only sound,
the sound of their bare feet in sand.

WHICH RAT FEELS CUTE
WILL ROGERS FAILED CHILDBIRTH
WARTS REVEAL FEMININE CHARACTER

I keep saying friends I've never met
are looking for me. With the ocean
on one side and buildings on the other
they come up behind. In my dream
they say, *None of it's clear.*
All of it's drunk.

We consciously don't judge
how far down the beach we've walked,
or why.

WITHOUT REASON FISH CHANGE
WE RADIATE FLIRTATIOUS CHARM
WOPSIDED RED FOLDING CHAIRS

This wandering the bars to find initials
willing enough to be a sentence
is throwing one collected handful
after another, a writing class from years ago,

people you run into, any random
assemblage, back
where they came from.

And each of us gets an award for doing so,
a tiny leather mail pouch, worn
on the left breast.

Arrive in the woods a late October afternoon,
put on the stove a big aluminum pot,
half full of water. Empty in the green peas
from their plastic sacks kept safe from mice,
with the rice, in the ironlidded skillet.

Walk upstream along the stream-path the real estate agents
Have not kept clear, lots of dead wood for starter.
discover a strange skinhole caveplace,
lizards living in and out the mouth, and something
bigger, the grass pushed down, a sliding-path.
Ferns brown now even before first freeze.

Walk back dragging long dead limbs. Scrape and wash
and chop six carrots for the mush. Soup on medium low,
walk the other way, with the creek, into the double spring
covered with waxy galax leaves, now getting on ground-foggy
dusk. A small dead tree needs pushing to break itself
and be guided down between its live kin and snaked home
through the rhododendron tunnel. Two rifle shots.

Meaningless tourist practice, puncturing beer cans
thrown to the far shore. Maybe some sweetnatured soul
yells from her kitchen, *Don't disturb the wilderness*
with that damn sniper-fire! They blessedly quit,
and here comes the scared big blue, low on the water.
Speak of blessings. Bow to the breathing flight,
wings go in, the body lifts breathing out.
Glide, and shudder when you read
of Lilith in her bird-form, screech-owl
sister to this, the day's grey-blue watery closing,
she the night-talons.

. . .

Can the need to be torn apart be soberly said?

Return to the soup. Slice green peppers,
undress and chop garlic. Undress onions.
Daub of butter shrinking in a skillet blacker
than any sky will ever be getting. Sauté.
Add these to these. More water, more curry, more
pepper. One more leg to the walk before full dark,
up iron steps along the road where powerline people
have been chainsawing, power I cook with
this minute. Here's a little pine tree
they left. Drag it back like Christmas.

Five whiting filets, cut in five pieces each.
Add a can of chicken broth, more curry, turmeric,
oregano, mucho file. Put the top
on the al-u-min-i-mum. Add to all week
the dearly loved heating-up-a-late-afternoon-
walk-soup-ceremony.

You with your soup spoon already in hand,
sit. Wait thirty minutes. Read. Be split open
for this we live. Is that the tearing needed?

Add this. One exhaustion knot
of wanting a woman off God-knows,
slow untangling of innards.

Is any man ready to marry Lilith?
Body's demanding beauty, Adam's first wife,
sexually willful, *I saw four guys today
that I would love to fuck.*

Who is here to marry that panic?
Put her raveling tendril-wandering
in your devotion soup. Turn off the stove.

Simmer clove and cinnamon stick
on a starlit walk in the icy creek,
nevermind your feet.

The moon comes up through the deeps
of water at your ankles, a smear of light
on the back of a stone.

And a barely visible nightbird swims away
in a sky that is nothing like soup,
free as a fireplace smoke,
no patient stirring around an axis of heat.

Driving eleven hours from Athens to Norfolk to see you,
I turn off and buy a basket of peaches
at a roadside place,
sit it on the seat beside me,
and look through the whole bunch one at a time.
It's like reading:

Patches of dark purple around the pole,
overlapping lights and darks, yellows and oranges,
mixing over the photographically dotted
globe. In my left hand,
this many versions of Jupiter.

Each peach has a seam,
as though it's been split open and sewn tighter,
no punctures on either side,
the perfect obstetric act. We imagine
what was taken out or put in. We bite
through the seam and try to think.

My mouth around and in you, my tongue
in the folds of the pit.
Don't leave your body. Stay here.
I start to cry, I'm waking up, I'm not,
but my head and my eyes feel
like they're crying.

This is the present I have brought you,
a basket full of planets, these fantasy women,
my overload of conceit.

. . .

Is it true, the myth, inside the pit
There is a hidden almond that's poison?
Is that the next tree, the next
face on the phone?

Two rockets leave for Jupiter this summer,
to fly close by, take eighty thousand pictures,
and spin off with new power, one to Saturn,
one to Uranus, both to deep space.

Sex has such a pull on me,
obviously, driving this far,
a two-way, equal and opposite,
pull: one out, speeding, the other
in, as the peach sweetly holds the pit,
and the pit holds tight to a secret bitterness.

I am taking a walk
on a cool, April morning through the cemetery
under the homemade archway gate.

The strength of the ants is pouring up
from under a slab, collapsing the edges
of a tireprint.

A singeing groundfire has been here.
Someone has lined up four seashells on one grave,
conch shells, saved from the ocean, placed
as if listening to the ground like the saying,
Keep an ear to the ground.

I empty one
by shaking and turning it to loosen the spiral
of dirt and sand.
I put my ear to its ear,
this valve for the ocean.

In the almost total quiet
I am wandering between the dead
and the dreamed, listening to a shell.

A slowmotion rainstorm
out on the ocean at night
blends and spends itself.

One love is that restful mixing
of freshwater and saltwater,
the great transparencies
inside each other.

*   *   *

Another love is work
the same as ants do, busy in the roots
of a live tree.

It hurts to look at them,
eating the mind and the imagination,
always at it.

Put your hands in the empty places.
Feel the ants along your arms.

Do the way the Ecuadorians weave Panama hats,
without looking, their arms underwater.

What is it we make here with the ants
in the subterranean wetness
and freshness?

New hats,
strong black hats,
composed of dirt and woven
with roothairs, a nest hat for each of us.

How is it so late? It's almost noon,
and I'm walking around in a daze.

Do you feel the ants along your arms?
People jealous and irritated with each other
for not giving enough time, people trying
to find something they want to do
this morning. Listen to yourself

saying, *Do what you feel like you have to.*
I don't care.

. . .

We are dizzy and sick
with such carelessness.

Once I was being chased
in a dream.

I hid in a woodshed,
where there was a mother goat.

They looked in.
I lay down and shut my eyes and sucked milk
from the goat's nipples.

The villains were so startled
they didn't recognize me.

I lay down and sucked milk
from a nipple.

I wish I did lie down like that
and get up without dropping a sip,
without missing a note or a leaf.
Last summer a man said to me,
You can't see it,
but there is a tree, long branches
reaching out.

The roots are in the ocean
of the mind. The tips are actual stars.

My children imagine how it might be
to swim in various substances:
think of motor oil.

Think of a swimming pool full of mercury.

.   .   .

Think of swimming in the milk
of a spirit tree: a cloud
where distance blends in the idea
of distance, light mixes with thinking
of light, burning, with love for the sun.

Graves, the singed pattern on the ground,
a seashell, the ants, air
in a moving tree.

Loud and soft voices lift and leave a room,
humming with themselves outdoors.

Two people with the lantern off
sit just a few feet apart, talking.
There's a slight wind.

One of the family legends
in our little group of five,
Mama and Daddy and Herb and Betsy and me,
is Dad's laughing all one night
after a speech he gave to the Rotary Club.

Dad was headmaster of a boy's preparatory school
for forty years and very serious
about the moral growth of the young,
but every now and then, at enormous intervals,
his trickster would erupt.

The subject was Education, of course,
and he had come across a very subtle satire
of self-important holding-forth,
a deadly treatise that sounded like
it was about something, but wasn't.

It was, in fact, similar
to the Monday afternoon chapel talks
he gave. He knew that and figured
a little Polonian high sentence
would amuse his peers at Rotary.

But no one got it. They sat politely
through one gust of fustian after another,
like church members at some imaginary
picnic on the North Atlantic,
holding their outrageous chapeaux.

•   •   •

And having gone so far, he had to bluff it
through, so as not to insult them,
and accept their heartfelt appreciation
for years of service and thoughtful
consideration of the issues.

He barely made it to the parking lot.
He hooted all the way home. We heard him
coming in, a noise somewhere between
the funniest joke and a howl
for his life spent mouthing maxims.

It was good, flat-on-your-back,
don't-nobody-have-a-clue, ocean laughing
and ocean weeping, and we tried to join him in it,
but nobody could.

He was hilariously alone
there in his bedroom, adrift
and at the mercy
of a profound audience
that kept swimming back by
in the wallpaper.

Where the filter of the hill
empties, I dig a miniature circular lake,
a foot across and a foot deep,
then leave to let it clear, come back
to arrange creek rocks around the edge,
and leave to let *that* clear and come back
to fill a mason jar and a coffee carafe
with spring water.

I have never been so slaked
with the mystery of freshness.

And now I have left for two weeks and come back
to find tiny spring lizards
living in the well-place I dug,
little waterbaby salamanders
under the sweetness of galax
and rhododendron around the opening,
that leads up through reticulated rapids
and invisibile passageways smooth with giving
the patience and hallucination
of groundwater into this mouth where
beings play in the clear
like tongues, like sounds that hide
so instantly, or pretend to hide.

Nothing can actually hide
its fear or its wiggly job
in so transparent a pool.

I come out of Bell's with a sack of stuff.
Leaning from the back window of a car
in the nearly empty lot is a child,

a boy-liveliness that a parent
might sometimes not-take
into the grocery store.
I have never seen him before.
"Hey!"
        "Hey."
                "Which car is yours?"

"That red truck over there."

"A man's been in it."

                "Oh he has."
"A man's been in it!"
He's pointing.

I touch his fingertip
with my free-hand forefinger
like the Sistine Daddy,

but rather the child
is power source here.

What do we want from any artist
more than that he change

. . .

the parked energy
to love-teasing?

With the help of what's missing,
to sail out a sentence
that opens the air.

I did not stay up till the end with my mother
the night she died. And here is the shame
from another vigil I did not make it completely
through, though shame is all wrong.

I told myself I would go from seven p.m.
to seven a.m., tending a fire, to watch and listen,
and I didn't make it. Sometime after four,
propped up, looking at the fire, resting my eyes,
suddenly it was six. The sun not yet up.

I immediately sat straight and began reading
Ramana Maharshi, hoping for some sort of spiritual hit
by dawn, though knowing the shame for falling asleep
is the same as the satisfaction of keeping a vow.

I felt refreshed by those two hours of dreamless doze.
Refreshment is a large service the universe offers,
and gladly accepted.

I heard, toward the ragged end of my vigil, what I took
as a degrading sign of failure, the toilet
left running, unjiggled, upstairs, the tank
with a balky gasket that needs coaxing,
or it won't re-fill enough
to stop re-filling.

I once came back from two weeks away
to hear that desertedness
in an empty house.

• • •

But now some sweet exhaustion absorbs
the sound with more than forgiveness,
and hears in its continuous emptying
a faithful pouring-listening
that never sleeps.

Fiesta Bowl on low.
My son lying here on the couch
on the "Dad" pillow he made for me
in the seventh grade. Now a sophomore
at Georgia Southern, driving back later today,
he sleeps with a white top hat over his face.

I'm a dancin' fool.

Twenty years ago, half the form
he sleeps within came out of nowhere
with a million micro-lemmings who all died but one
piercer of membrane, specially picked to start a brainmaking,
egg-drop soup, that stirred two sun and moon centers
for a new-painted sky in the tiniest
ballroom imaginable.

Now he's rousing, six feet long,
turning on his side. Now he's gone.

I sound low-key,
but this is the way I howl an old hymn
in the plaintive bass-drone,
a charm for accepting what happens,
and a stubborn question,

. . .

            in the
   why   *val-*
Say   *ley*
            of death should   *weep*
Or   *I*
   lone   *the*   *derness*
      in   *wil-*
            rove?

There's no one to worry about waking
with my singing. I have loved them,
those two boys, so well
that they've left.

We're after the fact now,
out in nowhere again.

We're I, and I am a line of music
wriggling along like water
wanting to be ocean.

     dars of Le-
  ce-   *ba*   *bow*
The   *non*   *at*   *feet,*
             his
        with his
The   *is*   *fumed*
  air *per-*
            breath.

Singing and talking,
one vibrates with the other.
Vapor-mist-going-up-this-way,
cloud-come-back-around-down.

  • • •

The old FaSoLa singers
would not commit to words,
until they ran through the notes,
in broken lines of rain.

The reverse of me rocking my babies
to all verses of Samnthra,
or *David's Lamentation,*
who now in a shower somewhere
murmur tunes they have no lyrics for.

La la   la
          sol   sol
     mi   mi   mi mi
               do

I never took them to church,
or told them stories about David,
or Samuel, or Jesus,
but they move like fish,
or tadpole-radios in the mud,
flat on their backs on a roof,
or breezing by.

Maybe any motion is holy music,
not only theirs.

Remember how it went,
then forget.

Sliding, forget more.

Sliding air in the throat, this song
it seems so soon to quit,
any shred of unfinished existence,

•   •   •

La la la
        sol sol
                mi

that somehow
is unbelievably over.

The growing
            of the
                    corn

over and over.

Our watery bodies keep moving.

   Hands give.
   Eyes weep.
   Feet walk.
   Shoulders swim.
   The throat sings.
   The chest hopes.
   The genitals wait.
   and the thighs,

their small-stroke dancing work of balancing and lifting,
the thighs,
                slow-move
a big riverlike forgiveness
we can jump in,
I and my strong boys, now men.

Some songs don't ever get completely sung.
They're sung by the blood,
inside creeks and rocks and air,

in some cellular Beulah land,
the harmonizing water sings them.

```
        do
    ti
fa          fa
      sol
          mi   mi              mi
                re
                  do      do
                    ti  ti
              la         la       la
```

Friends have brought me
to this schoolhouse in downtown Santa Cruz,
no longer a school, but a meeting place.
Darshan Singh and Sawan Singh devotees
in one room, say the second grade classroom,
and directly across the hall, an ecology
organization, a real estate office, and down
at the end the Whosoeverwill Mt. Moriah
Baptist Church is using the old fourth grade room
as their church this Sunday morning. Maybe
their building burned, or maybe they never had one,
I don't know. I'm down and across the wide,
worn, wooden-floor hall meditating
with seven Singh people.

When of a sudden, with no accompaniment, comes
the homesick sound of An Unclouded Day,
in the whinge and the whang
of a loudness I know.

  O the Land of Starry Skies
  Oooo the Land of an Unclouded Day
  Oooooo they tell me of a Land Far Across the Sea
  Ooooooooooooooooooooooooooooooo they tell me
  of an Unclouded Day

Floats me away. Do I want to be there or here?
Home, or home, or home, or home.

Where I'm from is some who I am.

. . .

As St. Augustine says, if what gets saved
is completely separate from my body, it's not me
that gets saved. Thence the doctrine
of the Resurrection of the Body.

My feeling is,

I can stay here subtle-Singhing,
or go to outloud, old-shoe singsong,
or buy some land, or save some wilderness.

It's all one fine, multipurpose meetinghouse
and temporary sanctuary,
with a silverplated sugar dish
on a white satin pillowcase
folded for an altar.

I'll visit them all,
and walk the hall,
singing my half-quiet song
in a bundle of tongues.

> *There are many rooms in*
> *this makeshift morning,*

> *And ways we've yet to let*
> *the schoolhouse be.*

For Mike Nicholson

Coffee
The oldest possible moon (left hand cups in the waning),
transparent sphere about empty,
the experiment done,
in a dawn-blue so close, walking,
I keep checking my eyesight against a huge pine
rising next to those apartments.
Resolution clear.

Coffee at the Waffle House,
Suzie runs me off by calling in company,
"Sir, would you like to join this fellow in the corner?"
They're too busy for me to take up a booth
with my vision-notes. *I'm just leaving.*

On the way home on the topmost strut of the pine
is a crow, in the first actual seen sun,
an important spot.

awe-awe   awe

A messy, whacking, lift-off,
then a smooth-measured exit in a curving diagonal
over my intention,
and below the gorgeous
exhaustion.

My friend Mike Nicholson is dying
of an odd bone marrow cancer and kidney thing.
Just my age. As I pass his house, there is one lamp on
in the kitchen, figures moving. He and Tanna

making coffee. A bubbling moon one morning,
the next three absent.

This one is quick, bitter, steamed-up life.
We get shooed out before we're finished.
Fifty, I still don't know when's best to get up,
and when to go to bed.

A spooked crow flies off in his animal sleep.
We walk to wake between various naps,
and one or two dyings.

I can't say what I feel.
I can't even feel it.

Mike is leaving early.
Is death better than being sick?

His eyes so wide and wondering, laugh so light.
"It's the medication, my friend,
chemical wisdom."

He's like a wonderful one-day Southern snow,
everything shut down. Everybody at home
on the phone.

Isn't it beautiful? It's so pretty.
I've been walking around in it.
Now I think I'll stay inside and read.
All the shenanigans I need
I can do from right in this chair.

The Second Mike Poem
I wrote your death-poem,
and you didn't die!

· · ·

It was right moving too, but now here
like the last speaker of a lost Indian tongue
you stand in your shroud of invisible laughter.

The story is:
                You were sitting at lunch chewing
the bitter facts, how kidney transplants
in Sweden work in half the cases. Half live,
half die.
            And if you had a kidney handy,
you might chance it, like the mumblety-peg knife
off the left shoulder for the third time,
Chance the Game, rather than live out slow
dialysis diminishment.
                        I can't stand the waiting room,
Coleman, those kids getting weaker every week.

Next to you, Rick Johnson says,
"You can have one of mine."
                            And he meant it,
and the tissues matched and it's DONE.
Coin flipped, called, the new potato's
pumping, filtering, protein-ing.
                            By sweet damn,
you're here for a while-bit! A while-bit,
little piece of flesh. Bless the doctors, bless
the tissue-ologists,, the analytic looks
down micro-tunnels, notes noted,
action: Cut, Sew, Mop
                    Laugh, Shake My Hand!

I don't understand what we are.
We are somewhat each other's fingers and voices
and eyes, as you are part-Rick now. Wave.
You-Who, match-mirror, through the glass.

. . .

We ride these flimsy bark canoes, talking
the upstream effort, and then the slide down,
poofing out air-sound at what seems a relief
within the overtone of an unseen drop-off,
getting louder, and funnier.
Where are we heading?
What are we saying
but a gladness for being?

A knife stuck in the ground,
and the ground held. Not forever,
whoever said forever?
I said forever.

While you were getting cut upon August,
I happened to turn to an Eliot poem. I never
read Eliot, except to teach him, and never this.
"A Cooking Egg." A stuffy, precious,
bad-laughter thing with these lines,

"I shall not want Honour in Heaven
    For I shall meet Sir Philip Sidney
And have talk with Coriolanus
    And other heroes of that Kidney."

Don't you appreciate a literary reference
in your resurrection poem? Your happy-come-on-home,
flowers-in-all-your-pockets poem. Smile for me.
I love Rick Johnson. Here's your picture
from the paper.
                Shitchyeah.
                        Mike, don't you like
walking around in a blue bathrobe with Sir Philip Sidney?
Ratty and royal blue.
                    Let's start a study group
at the Waffle House and do the entire corpus

of S.P. Sidney
          and other heroes
                  of that KIDNEY.
We've got time.
          I think they've lost my order.
                      Who cares?
I can wait all day for my precious egg,
                 just looking at you again,
so skinny and cantankerous
            and mean as a little bird.
I'm not even hungry.

Three
Now it's thrown back in our faces,
the acid of abscess and amyloid attack.

A month, and Rick's in an Atlantic clinic,
you're fading in Augusta.

I hear nothing but bad.
"It's been hell, buddy," you answer
the phone in intensive care.

They all tell us, the prophets,
that dying is like taking off a tight shoe
that you've worn all afternoon,
walking at the fairground.

Or much, much better. Flying inside music,
inside light. Snorkeling the indescribable reef
of the soul, the myriad niches,
                the pretty fitches.
You'll love it. I'll love it.

. . .

Let's get our signals right
before you roll over the side.

One pull is, *Hey, I'm here.*
Two is, *I love you all.*
Three is, *I'm loose and swimming*
in the joy of God.

Not that I have special information.
This is not so much belief as a big-time hope
they knew whereof they spoke, those old distributors
of these most delicious
                              loves and fishes.

Every Evening
I haven't done much with what's been given me
to do. I wander away and waste whole weeks.

Deathbed people scream, DON'T WAIT!
But I wait and waffle away
from clear warnings.

The cabin next door burns down
to a melted tire that could just as soon
be me. Mike may not make it
through Thanksgiving.

I love his fierce indignance.
Look at the damn wires.
We can hardly see the sunset.

He wrote a savage column last year
on mall architecture.
                              We haven't forgotten
what beauty is, but we have forgotten
to demand it!

And manning the Peace Booth
downtown: a smug young guy strolls up
with supposedly Christian slogans
for a bigger Pentagon.
                              Mike scrabbles
over the top like a bantamweight
going after the money changers.

To avoid suit, he had to endure a conference
in the fellow's pastor's polyester office.
Wonder he didn't chew the rug off the floor.
Wonder the minister's bookcase wasn't inscribed,

    Mene, mene, mickel Michael Nichol-
    Son, I love your quick goodness
    fighting at my peace table.

Don't wait to do what you feel here
to do. Obey the sudden truth.

Love the demanding beauty
of a bloodred late November sun.

Mike, let's crackle our imaginary walking
faster and brighter toward where that thing burns
inside its own and our sky-opened chest,
open to what death keeps beyond
us every evening.

The End of the Sentence
Home is where the art is,
without the he.

Home is where it's at,
without the her.

   . . .

Alison is a painter and a carpenter,
and my love-in-the-making, and those are
our unmarried marriage-songs.

We live and love thirty miles and minutes
apart. Separate homes, same his-and-her heart.

Last night I stayed with her in Lexington.
We tried to think of the sentence
Mike put on the wall at one of his showings.

"It's difficult to write a *Paradiso*,
when . . ." But we couldn't get the end.

"It's difficult to write a *Paradiso*,
when all the world wants is an epilogue."

Not bad, but not it. I drove back to Athens
this morning and went to look in on Mike.

He snoring away. Margot Rosenbaum is there.
"You writing much lately?"
                          "Well, yeah."
Mike opens his eyes.
                    "He's got a little telephone
by his bed that he listens to everybody's secrets on."

"I wish. Hey buddy, Alison and I were trying
to think of the end of your sentence,
'It's difficult to write a *Paradiso* . . .'"

When you're facing a conflagration.

.   .   .

"Right. We couldn't get it." He snores back,
days and nights reversed. The others leave,
and I sit there with the shades pulled.

The physical therapist slips in. "Do you think
he'll feel like some exercise later?"
                                        "Gosh,
I don't know. Can he get up?"
                                "We lift him.
He went over to the window this morning."

I woke at Alison's,
staring into the drowningly open
day.
      A band of birds
                        shot across the pane,
and I felt how Mike
won't see that much detail again.

On his walker all concentration goes
to the exhaustion of one foot.
He tries to attack.
                    "I don't know what
any of this means."
                    "I don't either."
"Where's the fairness factor?"
                                "I don't know."
"Why do you keep coming up here?"
                                    "I just like
to hang out. I don't know."

Outside in the air, I see a glory,
his searing, soaring honesty
lifting above my seed-picking.

        .   .   .

I need to attack myself.

He is the haw of human-ness
riding bright-cold winter.

I will never write anything else
about anybody's death,
and that's not what this is.

We don't die.
We just can't be
located quite.

The talk continues
on the secret phones.

Alison and I are so alone
that we can love. We have to have
privacy, and we have to have
the phone.

It's hard to claim to be living in *Paradiso*,
when you're watching a friend burn
down to an intricate ember.

Mike winked at me out of near-coma,
and sang a faint, madeup song,

> Coming to the Station O
> Coming early to the Station

Alison said, *Sweet Darling*.
We do die.
Harp upon it.

. . .

We end.
We miss.

And the spirit's true too,
a tenderness stringing us painfully,
almost hilariously, out of these skeletal
identities like chimney threads
into one blind longing.

The Fucking Grave
These last twenty days I have stood by the tomb
of Saint John, by the lost grave of Luke, a hillside
to point at, by the supposed forearm of John the Baptist.
I have walked into the last house of Mary Mother of Jesus,
into the mausoleum of Jelaluddin Rumi, my sheikh.

I have shown myself in his brass candlesticks,
and nodded to tough Shams Tabrizi, who knows I'm not
ready to work on his book, and seen country-dawn,
hardworking Haji Bektas, with his hand
flailing some outrageous truth,
the closest kin to this,
                    God's saint ranting
in my chest, not out of a newly filled-in
nothing-hole in the Oconee Hill Cemetery.

Don't be absurd. Mike touches now the wide wing
of all being and art, and wonders what
the cawhompus comes next.

Now you're talking!
Finish wrapping.

\. \. \.

I got home last night at four a.m. from Turkey,
gone there to see the dervishes turn.

At the Waffle House this noon
they tell me you died a week ago,
when as it happens, I was dreaming
that an old lover had died, and I had been
asked to find the right burial site.

I picked a place where she and I once
made love on the ground for the grave.

That was Mike in the spirit,
having fun with me, the *fucking*
grave, don't you see?

Help me finish this, friend.
Closure-clothes, to wind
it up, God bless it.

Kneeling and crying in the pantry,
wrapping Christmas presents,
I hear so close,
                    Finish taping the packages,
Coleman. The mail goes at six. Cry
for yourself. Your connection to God
could be much grander.
                    Grandeur!
The eighteeeeen thousand universes!
Those sufi terms, what you been re-phrasing,
pal, they ain't but half-wrong!

   (our laughter)

Is that what death is,
finally making love

in a way where gender
is fused asunder in some
surprise, switcheroo,
trainstation bed?

Whooooooooooooooooo
  aunnnnnnnnnnnnnnnnnnnnnnnnh
    Yoooooooooooooooooooooooooo

Salt
I hear me singing hymns,
full of fear and rosy pretending.

And this art and literature circus
is mostly preening and distraction.

I can crack Mike's whip a little,
since he's not here.

We need some salt
to get the truth more
grainy and bare.

We go out to buy our grown son a car,
a used one. We get down to look under it,
not knowing what we're looking for,
some burbling, viscous drip.

We're lying there on the ground in the car lot
when we realize we can't get up
without a lot of help.

* * *

That's a funny position to be in.
I do wonder how much of my "spirituality"
is fantasizing, though I would bet
this closeness *is*

a truth we come from
and thread back into,

like the freestanding waterfall
I saw once in a dream. (There's mystery
beyond betting in dreams.)

The waterfall flowed from the ground off a cliff's brow
and back underneath at its foot, visible
just in descending, standing
on its foamy nest, beginning and ending.

We are these pouring moments
of autumn water, as though a basin broke.

And there's no explaining
what gets stirred around
in the soup of our small talk.
We've just the taste.

———————

Who's in that corner booth?
Some old ghost.
He must be an illusion.

I didn't see him much last year,
and this year's not any better.
He must be part of my very soul.

· · ·

Look at that pigeon
looking at us. Makes me
feel like an aquarium.

Closed in,
to be stared at.

Endings want us to open out,
and not just trail off
the way I usually . . .

What I want
is like the woman I heard of
who dreamed a candle on her hospital
window ledge, down to its last.

The little wavering dance wen out.
Immediately, her vision shifted
through the dark window
to an outdoor, skyscraper candle
lit with a strong flame.

Though it's not some huge vision,
not an image of anything.

I won't know what I want
till I quit thinking
saying it is it.

The talk gets even smaller,
closer to silence,
then is.

Milton, the airport driver, retired now
from trucking, who ferried me
from the Greenville-Spartanburg airport
to Athens last Sunday midnight to 2:30 a.m.,
tells me about his son Tom, just back
from the Gulf War. "He's at Fort Stewart
with the 102nd Merchandized, the first tank unit
over the line, not a shot fired at them.
His job was to check the Iraqi tanks
that the airstrikes hit, hundreds of them.
The boy had never even come up on a car accident
here at home, twenty-four years old. Can you
imagine what he lifted the lid to find?
Three helmets with heads in them staring
from the floor, and that's just one tank.
He has screaming flashbacks, can't talk about it
anymore. I just told him to be strong
and put it out of his mind. With time,
if you stay strong, those things'll go away.
Or they'd find a bunker, one of those holes
they hid in, and yell something in American,
and wait a minute, then roll grenades in
and check it and find nineteen freshly killed guys,
some sixty, some fourteen, real thin,
They were just too scared to move.
He feels pretty bad about it, truthfully,
all this yellow-ribbon celebrating.
It wasn't a war really. I mean, he says
it was just piles and piles of their bodies.
Some of his friends got sick, started vomiting,
and had to be walked back to the rear.
Looks like to me it could have been worked
some other way. My boy came through OK,
but he won't go back, I'll tell you that.
He's getting out as soon as he can.

First chance comes, he'll be in Greenville
selling cars, or fixing them. He's good at both.
Pretty good carpenter too, you know how I know?
He'll tear the whole thing out if it's not right
and start over. There's some that'll look
at a board that's not flush and say *shit,*
nail it, but he can't do that, Tom."

The sweet tone of our desiring
on the phone, Rachel, is I want us
to lie down and kiss, or breakfast
out in the sun at the restaurant
near the P.O. Do you feel
me feeling this?

Lana Turner, love goddess, whom I notice
here in the *Toronto Star*, is seventy.
Her first movie, a bit-part walk-on
in *A Star Is Born*, 1937, came the year
I was born. Her story is mine.

We're discovered in the Top Hat maltshop
across from Hollywood High wearing this trademark
sweater, which we never took off, not for a one
of our seven husbands and a slough of real
and publicist-invented romancers.

No critic ever took her seriously.
This is also true of me.

Real-life drama came to Lana
when her teenage daughter, Cheryl,
stabbed to death Lana's hoodlum-lover,
Johnny Stompanato, who was threatening
to disfigure Lana. Cheryl was cleared
on grounds of justifiable homicide.

Maybe some violence threatened me too
in the early fifties, that I didn't understand
my role in, and can't recall repressing.

Then came 1957, and while Lana was Oscar-nominated
as the steamy mistress in *Peyton Place*.

I am taken to bed by three TWA stewardesses
in the luckiest string of summer nights
ever threaded upon bare, forked being.

Is it repulsive, or funny, or just a marvel, how we
peak and moon around and change partners,
and wonder why we went where?

Nothing much since.
One season on *Falcon Crest*.

Lana resides now on the twentieth floor
of a posh LA highrise with two large terraces
as exquisitely shaped as her breasts
used to be, turning their one hundred eighty
degrees from the desert to the Santa Monica Pier.

It's her ivory tower, and since 1969
she has been quote "celibate by choice.
I am very close to God. I read the *Daily Word*,
and I have learned to meditate. The age-thing
is just a bunch of numbers." Unquote.
I couldn't agree more.

Rachel, I get smoothed and here,
with you coming toward me,
on the phone or in flesh.

The plane is taking off this second.
You may not tolerate my silly-Lana.
So make me honest. I know another
beautiful Rachel, a Rajneesh sannyasin
who has written a very trying-for-truth book
called *The Orgasmic Mirror*, a journal
of spiritual feelings and sexual connections.

* * *

She and I are not lovers. Shall we
share erotic tanglings, you and I?
Who else but us will ever read this?
If the phrasing's good, many.

Would I trade what and who I want
for beautiful language that holds the desiring
and a little of its satisfaction?
Do I have to choose? Can't I have both?

How will men and women be more open in ten years?
Keep those predicates jiggling, camerado.
We're slanting into Cleveland.

I want to unwrap you, button by
button, by snap, by zipper. I want
to nurse your nipples. My desire wants
inside yours and then to change,
saying the shifts as we go.

I see Lana meditating
with a coffee maker drippling
nearby, her eyelids identical
to the Buddha on her vanity.

And now going out for a semi-reclusive lunch,
salmon sauce, spawning hunger spread over
her reaching into some table condiment.

In Cherokee the question is,
"How deep is your well?"
Not "How's it going?"
the car metaphor.

I want our native wellsprings mixing,
but I don't want to live together, or help

raise your little girl, though I love her.
I have raised two children, more or less,
but could we see each other more?

And I don't want to hurt your husband's feelings.
I don't want him to know. For God's sake,
these *I don't want's*. I don't want
to covet another man's wife, but I do.

Is there a way of wisdom wherein
there are no secrets, where these and those
won't matter? My noggin feel stroke-prone.

I'll tell you now a story that makes me crazy,
high over my country of origin.

My nephew Daniel became a fighter pilot,
because he didn't play football at the fiercely
footballed school we all went to, where
for three and a half months every year
from the seventh to the twelfth grade
we put on pads five days a week and blammed
each other in a galloping hormonal joy,
spent the aggression and the fear, did what
passed for heroics that didn't kill anybody,
and became great, relieved buddies.

Daniel didn't do that. He learned tai chi
and meditative calisthenics, so that
at twenty-six he had not gone through as much
careening bump-ass as needed, and had to
put himself through the scariest regimen
he could find, which was to land
Navy jets on carriers at night.

He did it the best of any in his class,
and then this Bush-Saddam madness arrived,

and he was sent, not as a pilot, but as
a high-level liaison with the Saudis.
He was right there in the Riyadh war room,
and as January 15th approached, the old
commanders recognized that the quickest
gun they had was Daniel. They put
his lightning reactions up in an AWACS
and told him to direct the whole show.

When the Red Sea F-16's, when the far, land-based
B-52's, now the Brits, now the Stealth, and come on
you A-6's from the Gulf. For the first two weeks
of fighting he called our four-dimensional
square dance of death.

They sent him home early.
We had a family welcome dinner,
but he couldn't say anything yet,
where he'd been what went on.
He hadn't been debriefed.

He looked straight at me: "This war we do now
is not about making warriors." His laugh
was strange, and he drank a bunch
of martinis to no effect.

Whatever's-in-charge has damaged Daniel's
animal gladness, diminished his grief,
and given in exchange the Bronze Star.

What do I get? Dollar gas? Cat got
your tongue? I have a tongue-eating
Iraqi housepet I'm sitting.
Don't touch her.

Next to my phone is a list of culture sites
in Baghdad, which back in early January

I was going to write a magazine article on,
with color pictures, so we could see some
of what was there, before we destroyed it,
unlike Hanoi, which nobody knows what
it ever looked like, but I was way too slow.

The tomahawks were already lifting from their racks.

1. The Al-Gilani Mosque for Abdul Qadir Gilani,
   my teacher's teacher's teacher's teacher.
   I go that way back, and other ways too.

2. The mosque on the spot where al-Hallaj
   Mansur was martyred in 922 A.D.
   for saying, "I am the Truth."
   Hallaj, godalmighty.

I won't continue naming the twelve jewels.
I'm too slow, but I know this
is a deep well, Rachel, where everything
dissolves into love poem.

Feed me. I need your milk. Take off
your shirt. I need to suck skin
as if it weren't imaginary.

We are not seventy yet, or celibate.
Wantings change, and we begin
to see what's in them.
Which way now?

Lana's real name is something else,
we learn at the end.

. . .

Who am I? Am love and truth and confusion,
and a lost bear trying to walk along
with several angry sweethearts.

Do not fuck your life up because of me.
This cultural anger and eros dance
may not be one you feel led to join.

It is mostly a waiting. For what or whom,
I do not know. Rip Van Astronaut
sits atop his gantry twenty years
dreaming ignition. My psychoanalyzing
of Daniel and his humbly efficient pilot-buddies
may be more saying I am skipping exercise
that could calm this shadow-rage.

And/or it may be true that young men feel such pride
of mastery in their machines that they lose
compassion and cannot imagine anymore
the shredded organs their ordnance feeds on.

Never enough. Daniel will write his Iraqi memoir,
as Rachel her own account of love's fumbling.

Because writing is also waiting,
like this, full of hurt laughter and wanting
a new double love poem, meeting in the come-close,
come-close, then repair to separate balconies.

Because it is not you now, Rachel,
and it is not Iraq. Desire and anger
switch to quicken elsewhere in the months
or year I have fiddled with and forgotten,
this trying to get them down in language.

. . .

I tender words to see if after a while
They will toughen to a shape.

No sexual trance is what waiting is for,
no being with another dying being.

Can it be it's not getting laid,
or living with a true love?

There are things to do,
other than exchange juices.

My breathing bumbles and disrupts.
I am not Lana. These next fifteen, secret years.
Give me a good quote, Miss Turner.

I want sexual excitement, but less and less.
I want my breath to stay deep and strong,
to feel some risky truth moving there.

Because beyond this poosh, and the back in,
a heard-shape of nightwater rushes by,
the emptying flume of mystery
that I have seen in one person, and is
what I long to have come flooding through,
so that the waiting will be less and more
a helpful hingeing out into sun, or folding
into a room, however is needed for faces
gazing back, the being whose water
of presence washes around us.

Mistrust and lying, jealousy and some desire,
feel closed off. Live inside the listening
conversation that is our joy and art.

. . .

In what my new love from Toronto
says and does I hear the gift again.

Though we don't seem to want to be together
for more than a month at a time. We go
back and forth, splitting airfares.
We have no rules but to stay
conscious and honest.

Which is a lot, and we are not
very successful so far.

I am fifty-five and have never tried this
with a woman. I'll hush. *Faithful*
and *unfaithful* are these ribbed cloud-racks,
so many soluble compositor trays
I descend through, this surrender afternoon.

Nothing to obey or disobey.
What I feel, who and if to live with,
are not known certainties for long.

I wait and act and say and write things
for the energy and dissolvings
love seems to require.

Rain-listening sluice, well washer,
hurler of horse troughs against the roof,
waterbody rising unnameable over the meadow-slant
to burrow every secret storeroom of yellow jacket nest,
dissolve to Turkish mud-dauber caves under the joists,
fill the shallow pewter spoons of the horseshoe pits
with ringing silence, and for one moment film the deck,
soak the rug level with these insoles, unfooted
and footed, and through each eyelet caress
the skin arch of who sits alone reading,
with now no light, the unheard transformer blown,
to hum and slightly list-lift the house-bubble
three inches downstream, no more, certain warning
and smothered applause. The spices jostle watching
from their three aristocratic rack-balconies,
some wanting to flavor such a huge soup with paprika
and oregano, some to just stand unopened,
the cardamom, the anise seed, the dried rosemary,
for there will be no delicate enhancing of taste,
the while this confusion covers the first shelf,
smoothing the mystical spine of Gregory over
Niffari's visionary shreds and into Sanai's
gateless garden pool, the overflow-memories
immediately detaching from their fictions, where
the melted cup came from, why a one-button-eyed bear
sits with a snake-crick and an oddly triple-racked
budvase, how this iron skillet followed innertubes
through the rapids one August afternoon, wobbling
its shoulders through the boulders, and would not
be sunk, foundering to some use now unrecalled,
like this broken-off stalagtite compacted of slow-tears,
and the second shelf with its Eskimo healing chants
and Taoist drinking songs, and my mother's college
English Romantic poetry anthology underlined
in red, and now my thighs suddenly peninsula

toward the third, a line of Russian novels
and the Machu Picchu picture book. This is how
everywhere comes at once into being, sopping
bookprint to an unreadable paste,
with the bridge crossed quietly two miles downroad
plunging past so close, an enormous swimmer
made of telephone poles, flopping odd angles
to the flow, a monstrously drowning dumbshow
of what's not been loved enough, the failure seen,
and then there is peace in water-patches,
one of them circular, balanced around my collar bone
like an antique Dutch wedding costume,
that because I never put it on, returns for
a new rehearsal where furniture cuts loose,
and endtables romp to the door, and my mouth
fills with an unblinking, no-longer-thirsty rose
opening its silken hallway above my forehead,
the passion I swim within, a new creature
slipping through the dark water,
shaped like a normal breath, a trout-joy
exploring what begat and will re-absorb, a slim
alleluia cruising the sunk fridge, and effortless
mandorla round the carpentry edges of the counter
like a worker's hand fiddling rearrangement,
a faint glow of decision, parting slightly
the sliding glass where morning begins
its earliest spring flower pranks,
the turtle-streaked music of dawn, with these lips
a mere hole mouthing an invisible breast,
the lure of a flooded throat when the sun comes
nudging through a fine lawn of marine distinctions,
its face: am fish, am drowned man, am-am-not
seated on the ground like a bust of Hermes
at a crossroads protruding in this taken-in
and given-back water to read aloud a line
of scummy leaf-bits sticky enough to adhere,
while all the other runs with whoever wrote

this chair-rail of Tibetan twig-cypher: is,
could, into the going will, does, are,
gone, and here, and there, let remain
as remains, a muck-statue of me speaking
the first verse of its debris song,
that has only the one, "I must stand up
and see what works and what doesn't, start
cleaning, must stand and start, must, must,
can't, must . . ." and so on the mud-verbs spell
around the side of the house, everything in it
lonely for singing-breath. Take me with you!
Naked again, and bringing more naked invitees
to the hopeless expungement of wall and floor,
lead us all *out* wherever you swim
your swift enthusiasm, sleek, wivvery,
sunflower seeds of a schooling choir,
deep-pooled under a roaring event-roof,
full-shivering sliders into a nativity
that accepts everything, water of life, being
with known and unknown others under
the force of discourse in sweet community,
and as well paralyzed in a sodden armchair,
and as well escape itself, scintillae
scattering on a stirred surface, as those there,
the lake-lovers lying on their backs pointing,
become meteors, and Cassiopeia slides
through the hemlocks. Sand and small rocks
clog the toaster while dawn down-comes
inside the liquid light-kissing fingertips
lifting the fogfed, thinning juice-door
onto the washed scene. Many voices
in cahoots: am eye am, can tell how the table
puts down one leg before another, and silt
settles from within its ash-fibbling layerage,
can watch the water-inhabiting motion take
other shapes, leave the digression covered with
a fuller's earth of the most unfortunate good

luck to have a creek near enough
to rise overhead that now recedes
to a more measured sound, a plucked-string,
fretted and released body, banking back into
an almost obeyed grammar, the patience
and ordinary agreement of rock resisting water,
can hear from out in the Sargasso eel-squirm,
a couple talking, and be both. Pooling
and evaporating eddy-niches expand
to a bland and obvious pond. Forms of
forgetting and waterfalling spontaneity mix
with sky to become the fascination tremendans
coursing through, this coldness my whole head
dips beneath, called Fightingtown, *Un-ul-sti-yi*
in Cherokee, a cleared place, a chief
skilled at village-against-village,
and the quick river that ran in my house.

I invite you again and again, but you are not
the streaming I long for. You dribble
your drop on mine, and we wed,
wanting greater deluge.

There is one book, a 1988 volume,
and it is here, never been checked out,
and flipping through, I sniff the carefulness,
the guarded assertions this Oxford guy
spent twelve years considering, so that now
I can have the rest of a spring afternoon
finding out what is known and what
will remain secret a while longer
about the Sixth Dalai Lama.

Good scholarship gives me such delight that I kiss
the book alone in the stacks, and I almost kiss
the checkout girl, and I savor the length
of the bibliography walking through
the self-opening double-doors, and I skip
going back to my truck, because Michael Aris
has sustained his interest in Tibetan mystics,
and I want to kiss the bald pate of research
like a n'er-do-well daughter going out on a date,
who before leaving, thoughtfully brings
some green tea for a little break.

for James August Pennington

I think the first poem I ever got was one by Edna St. Vincent Millay that
Mr. Pennington read our eighth-grade Latin class in (Good Lord!) 1951.
It's called "Afternoon on a Hill."

> I will be the gladdest thing
>   Under the sun!
> I will touch a hundred flowers
>   And not pick one.
>
> I will look at cliffs and clouds
>   With quiet eyes.
> Watch the wind bow down the grass
>   And the grass rise.
>
> And when the lights begin to show
>   Up from the town,
> I will mark which must be mine,
>   And then start down.

I was fourteen at the time and had grown up as a kind of joyful solitary
wandering the Baylor hill. I knew those cliffs and clouds, and I had looked
with quiet eyes. For the moment, *self* and *world* came together in *words*. I
still like the poem, though the first stanza seems inflated. Too sticky-sweet
for my taste now.

But O, I can still respond to the center of the poem, the grass and the
wind part. There is a phenomenon in human experience that needs a
name. Some have called it the *hieros gamos*, the sacred marriage, a kind
of glistening in the consciousness. Calm, trembling times when we feel
a deep sense of harmony with the soul. It is part of the work of artists to
find images and expressive form for that..

. . .

I am happily snowbound in the north Georgia mountains as I write this (Sunday, April 5th, 1987) and hear suddenly the ten inches of snow slide off one whole side of the A-frame roof. A slow, undertowing sound, almost as though it's inside me, but the dog has her ears up. Each of us discovers different ways of welcoming the universe into us, of being less and less defended against the warmth of the sacred marriage. Poetry became one of my ways. My brother Herb has riding the whitewater of the Chattooga as one of his. That is what the Greek term means. It is something essential and exciting, what I felt in Pennington's class.

Ecstatic, pure-being moments are not, of course, the whole story. There is irony and wit, reason and clear-eyed judgment, and the grounded ramble of an ornery human voice. There is Pennington's mighty opposite in those years, Jim Hitt. But what I, and others, learned from Pennington were *moments*, and the way sometimes words and the world will sing together.

Pennington could recognize those sacred-marriage, St. Vincent Millay grasses when he saw them shining in a Latin phrase, in the elegant condensation so possible in Latin. When Herb called and left the message on my machine that Mr. Pennington had died, I went to my old Virgil book and opened it at random. Now, there is some precedent for doing this. After Virgil's death it was a common practice, called the *Sortes Virgilianae*, to consult the works of Virgil to learn the future. On and off the practice continued, even into this century. The British High Command consulted Virgil for advice in WWI! (Pennington would love this scholarly aside!)

I open to page 474. It's book VI of the *Aeneid*. Aeneas is getting a glimpse of the other world. The only phrase circled on the page, in my 1955 scrawly pencil script, is *Hac iter Elysium nobiss*, which means, "This way takes us to the Elysian Fields (the sixth heaven)." How wonderful and incredible.

This is how it might have gone in the longago classroom.

.   .   .

"Which words did this guy Virgil choose to put next to each other?"

Silence.

"*Iter* and *Elysium*," he screams.

("Iter" is our word "itinerary.")

"What is he saying?" Pennington climbs us and is now standing on his desk.

More silence. Pennington descends and circles the room, prowling, pulling shirts up, untucking ties. "What is he saying?"

"The trip feels heavenly." Borisky feels brave.

"You would." Borisky's shirt gets unbuttoned two buttons.

"Go for the gold!"

"Hey, take a round off, Seessel, yehhhhhhhh."

"The journey is the kingdom." My try.
Long pause.

"You know, Coleman, I think so. I think soooooooooo."

(I was his favorite, some days.)

He sits back down in his tilt-back chair, relieved, and tilts way back.

"Oh, young men, I love woids, woids, wooooiiiiddddds."

. . .

Arms open, shivering upward, "Iter Elysium!"

Over his classroom door, as you went out, was the sign,

   HAEC OLIM MEMINNISSE IUVABIT

Hereafter, it will have been pleasant to have remembered these things.

Haec Olim. Yell it, *HAEC OLIM!*

These things hereafter, Mr. Pennnnnnyyyyyyyyyyy.

As I look up the Millay poem to check how closely I remember it—
close enough—here on the opposite page is another poem of hers that I
remember Pennington loving:

   Lord, I do fear
   Thou'st made the world too beautiful this year;
   My soul is all but out of me,—let fall
   No burning leaf; prithee, let no bird call.

Such an extravagant heart, Edna Millay, and James Pennington, in his
moments, was more than a match for her.

for Harold Parrish

First calendar day of winter I drive up to the mountains, sleet-slushy
roads, and don't make it, leave the truck with its passenger-side load of
books and groceries and wine a mile and a half back at a turn-off place
and walk in with one plastic bag of bargain chicken thighs. It is supposed
to warm up tomorrow. Chicken on low, with every spice and herb I own,
smelling wonderful, even red pepper. Two years ago a poetry student of
mine who went on sort of aimlessly to English graduate school—you
could not imagine him teaching a class, very withdrawn and reckless and
sweet—would come to my office and stand around while I was work-
ing, blurting out anything self-consciously strange and giggling like he
did when he read his poems. *Why don't vampires dress in plaid?*—has
been found frozen to death in his car. He had been drinking and passed
out behind his father's house, neglected to go in and get to bed one real
cold night. I have checked out his master's thesis from the departmen-
tal office and have it here in the cabin. Some service is due him, some
notice. Some blame attaches to me. We used to have a poetry group when
he was an undergraduate. We drank too much red Gallo, and I should
have warned him away from graduate study that couldn't lead anywhere,
that made him depressed and frustrated. I have heard he had been look-
ing for a job for two years before he died. No openings, so he had gone
back to stay with his parents in Rossville. Everybody called him Parrish.
When you met him in the hall, you'd say "Parrish," louder than need be,
and he'd smile and nod elaborately. His thesis is about the wedding-feast
in the Middle English poem, *Cleanness*, or *Purity*, which was bound in
the *Gawain* manuscript. One invited guest to the banquet has torn and
messy clothes, an allegory for the impropriety of spiritual carelessness in
the presence of the Lord. Parrish, himself famously scruffy, writes well
about that filthy figure. Fallen man, saved, invited to the feast, goes, but
in old clothes, still pleased with sinning. The misty sleet slicks and seems
to clean everything tonight. Even this near-to-rotten shard of plywood I
bring in to burn is a gleaming gift, enameled. Emanuel. In dream recently
Parrish was barkeep and keeping the bar open after closing time to let
me have a special beer and tell me of his new love, Jessica Savitch, the

newslady. We try to find her address in the phonebook on *Lila* Drive, and do. I realize that I too am in love with Jessica Savitch and had not realized it until now, but I don't tell Parrish and won't interfere. We go to the ridge where she lives where there is a school where everyone learns how to *praise*, constantly honoring the glory of God. Parrish says he doesn't think he has much chance to court her with that kind of competition around. End of dream. One way I clean up is to buy an empty book to keep a weather-and-other-natural-observations journal in: December 21st, low 20s. An inch of sleet this afternoon starting around 2:30, misting crystals till midnight, great slender lozenges of ice on the creek, ten, twenty feet long. Midnight to 10 a.m. a warm, Gulf-of-Mexico drizzle comes and makes the ice-sheathing drip and turn loose. Simple notation to balance my dream obsessions. I have napped many a time between towns on the carseat with my pony-express satchel for pillow, sleeping off each successive night's ragged enthusiasm. Learn what I seem to have great difficulty learning: there is a bright-cold sobriety, a steady calm sleet, that includes every possible drunkenness. Don't get tipsy with the wine of beings loving being, that song. More times, wait for clear pin-sounds to touch leaves and grass and railing and roof. In this allegory, cleaning means watching and listening, *tk-tk-tk-tk-tk*, quiet everywhere-noticing, not the celebration-recuperation cycle I have had enough schooling in. Parrish, I am soberly iced-in with you, my bottles of Rhine more than a mile away up the unwalkable road, cooking a wedding banquet for one, practicing a purity we ought to have been teaching each other ten years ago. December 22nd—up to 48 at 5:30 in the afternoon, light rain, grey-green overcast all day. Truck unstuck from iciness and unloaded, now stuck again in mud halfway up the hill, trying to drive over to check the mail. Harrold Parrish had sorrows and foolishness I played no part in, but I could be a lot more conscious and helpful than I have been. Parrish sleeping into death on the carseat reminds me how important every minor word we have with anyone is. Backsliding, fishtailing, and the road covered with crystal.

for James Wright

There is a sort of shed he had built he calls his brain-house. On con-
crete blocks, with carpeted floor, wallboard, electricity. He goes there
to write whatever comes. In the mountains beside a creek, with the
creeknoise so loud you can barely talk. He goes out early this morning,
unhungover, having been a good child to his soul last night, to write on
his yellow legal pad or type on his Royal, he thinks, but he cannot sit
still. He feels too good. He dances some sliding dance steps up and back
along the narrow floor. He sings something he does not have words to,
ummmhmmmmmm whumtoopootee poopah, ta. I say he when I mean
myself, or anyone before he knows for sure what he is dying of, say cancer
of the intestine. Before any symptoms. No tests have been run, no x-rays.
He is in his brain-house so dumb and happy he cannot settle down to do
any work, so he writes funny letter-notes to his friends. James Wright is
dying, for certain, these days in late February and March 1980. Cancer of
the lymph and throat, mouth and tongue. I have never met him except
through what we wrote. Those ponies he stopped with a friend to pet one
late afternoon by the highway, and the Sioux Indian with a hook for one
hand in the bus station in Minneapolis, who gave him sixty-five cents to
get home on. Small kindnesses he took some pains to record, because of
the many different ways, he knew, we go away from each other, then try
to come back with a phonecall, or very like a phone ringing. Now I sit
in the comfortable reading chair I have lugged up to this chamber, and
try to begin this other dance, the one the bright-sun daylight, even if it
were a man or a woman, an old friend standing in the door, could not
see me do. I have heard James Wright had a photographic memory. He
has been known to stand on a chair in a small entryway in Ann Arbor
and recite the whole of Byron's *Manfred*. With no one listening much at
the party, but there he is saying it without the book. I learn so slowly not
to be careless and wasteful. Be mindful, I pray to myself this afternoon,
with memories disappearing, detail lost. My father's recall totally gone,
along with James Wright's incredible *Manfred*. Right after lunch, when we
had learned that mother had died. Dad sat in his armchair and looked at
me. *I feel like hollering, if I thought it would do any good.* He didn't, but he

did die six weeks later, instantly, of a massive stroke, as though he could choose to do that. I am not one to scream either, but there is a scream inside me, and a stroke. Knowing and not-knowing, creeknoise and the other. I would like to get something done in the midst of this. Throw the camera at where the surf exactly hits the bottom of the cliff. I want the event and the memory of it to come even with each other, and there they would be, standing on the doorsill, together.

for Milner and June Ball

Out in the meadow beside the house to give coffee water time to boil, to check closer on the Carolina Silverbells in bloom that friends had identified for me yesterday, so I can say their names too when I see them somewhere else, here's a big turtle like a so obviously placed gift package where I couldn't possibly miss it, right in my no-path through the tall weeds. The hinged front third of his bottom plate closes with a wet hiss as I pick him up. Thirty minutes closed on this wooden table with me, coffee cup and spiral notebook, he opens a half-inch, puts one back-right, black-lagoon suit, lizardfoot down, eases his phenomenal, strong head out from under the eaves. No eyes. They are thickly cataracted over with layers of film. He tries once with the back of each foot to clear his vision, like a cat washing. He does have the clean, minutely drilled, twin holes of his nostrils. He stretches and points them in three directions. Now he lunges quickly away from me off the edge of the table. I catch him. He can see slightly out of his left eye. When I am within arm's reach of an animal, I think of St. Francis. Animals gauge my restlessness. I want them more comfortable with me than they are. St. Francis, so empty of fear and hasty nervousness the birds would light on him. Turtles probably wouldn't slam shut when he picked them up. I put this one back where I found him/her—him, there is the small dent in the stomach-plate for balancing in the act of copulation—and go on trying to identify Silverbells. Trunk and branches small and misty like dogwood. Why learn the names? If I don't, this place remains a green fog in my mind. I'm told the spirits sometimes do not know who they are at amateur séances, when they are called forth by someone not ready to do that. You ask, "Is this Shakespeare? Aunt Edith?" And the spirits say yes, because they are in a blurry limbo where they actually are nobody, and everyone. Names do matter. The Druids had a tree alphabet that has been lost, but evidently, in it, each letter denoted the essence of a particular kind of tree—the hemlock, the black tupelo, the white oak. Think of spelling words with those reminders of tree-essence. It is friendlier to have signs for the clear and separate beings of plant and amateur botanist, each living spirit like St. Francis. These blossoms here are white, hanging straight down, little

Tiffany Victorian reading lamps. The turtle is out walking again, already, with his misted-over, translucent will, and his lefthand slit of place coming through one eye. I read about St. Francis and trees, and then there is this figuring *work* to be done. I might have thought one time that classifying was distancing. There is some separateness to naming. But past thumbing through *Southern Trees* to page eighty-four there is this Black Tupelo (I think), with me for months, and now I have a term for this presence. Did St. Francis know the names? Probably not. He knew nicknames and spirit-names. It takes so many forms. Studying the differences is trying to join with that clear sap of intelligence, a kind of show-off devotion, while we wait for the true word to open.

for Johnny Thrasher

Five weekends now I've come up here, been told the water's fixed, and
five now it's busted, five, or fifteen minutes after I've crawled up under
the house to turn it on, this time only a quarter-turn. I hear a whang
and it's broken loose somewhere else. I crawl back and turn it off and
spend the weekend again without facilities. I know what's worth writing
about. What the heart—and I know we can't use that word very success-
fully anymore to mean the loving the self has in it, let's say it anyway—
what the heart remembers, what the mind is sometimes so attentive and
attuned to that it carries it in its pocket from then on. Anything might
be reduced to that handy size, the Matterhorn for example, a cameo of
Confucius. I don't deserve to get mad about this water business. I have
never plumbed a house. I call Johnny Thrasher and say this water's broke
loose again. He says *Ain't that a shame. I'll git up ther Monday afore work.*
He does good work. I've just got some trashy cheap piping under there,
garden hose he calls it, put in by the previous owner. *I'll put some PVC in
there fer ye, new fixtures in the kitchen and bathroom. It's all jist rotted to
rust and crumbling. Two hunnert and fifty dollars, and I'll guarantee it.* He
doesn't want to mess with what I've got any longer. I might try crawling
up under there to see what I could do, after watching him a few times, a
few hundred times. I might buy a chemical toilet and bring in drinking
water in water bags, not take baths and t'hell with it. I tell him, let's tear
it out and go in with the PVC. He's a great buddy now, drops in a Satur-
day morning, already glowingly drunk, 11 a.m., with his wife Ruth, whose
grandmother was a full-blooded Cherokee. *Works perfect, don't it. Looky
here, washerless faucets. I tole you we could git it right.* I am very thank-
ful for Johnny Thrasher. I have plenty of other things I can do here by
myself, other than writing I mean, physical, survival work for the precari-
ous fleck of consciousness that is this house. Hauling rock in the wheel-
barrow to bolster two concrete block piers that the stream is beginning to
lick underneath when it rises. I can spend the entire summer hauling rock
to make that bank secure. The work here is watching water, containing it
some. The movements and sound: thrummings exactly like a bass drum,

a low dragging noise like a heavy glass door sliding open. I return to the deck and look down through the intricate presence of Fightingtown Creek, named for the Cherokee chief, Fightingtown. Ruth says, *They's supposed to be gold and Indian things buried along this creek. Maybe you'll find something, if you keep digging up rocks.*

for Jordan, who helps wash them

About gourds, one thing they say in Blue Ridge is, "It takes a fool to grow a gourd," and they notice how I always get a good crop. The other thing they say is that you have to hard-cuss gourd seed as you put them in the ground. To get their attention before they'll even consider coming up. Gourds are stubborn-stubborn. In the mystical poetry of Jelaluddin Rumi gourds are a metaphor for human beings, and their rattling speech. If we make our noises against enclosure long and hard enough, we'll break out and have some chance to germinate. This is the process: planted in mid-May, a gourd vine becomes a wildly growing thing through July. I have clocked one tendril on a wet and sunny summer afternoon at one and a half inches every two hours. The entire vine grows seven yards a week. Of the kinds I know, one flowers white, opening in the evening, the other yellow, opening in the morning. Where the flowers drop off, fruit nubs appear and swell and streak and fill with rain. In the middle of September you bring these heavy young-uns in and lay them side by side on newspapers on the daybed, where they can rot. When they get good and mildew-black with fur, you take them to the picnic table and wash them in white vinegar, scraping off the scum with your fingernails, leaving designs. After another month they'll fuzz up again. Take them back to the table with the vinegar and hold and wash and caress them like babies. Then do it again. You'll have dirty fingernails and hands that smell vinegary and some fine hardshell gourds. People, of course, make marten houses and soup ladles and fancy African instruments out of gourds. Some friends brought me a Balinese penis-sheath that is a long-handled dipper gourd cut off where the handlepart enters the womb cavity. Me, I shake them to loosen the seeds from the clump inside and give them away whole on Gourd Day. Why can't a person make up a holiday and a way to celebrate it? It is December 17th, around sunset, with the sky deep winter red, that I secretly tie gourds to my friends' door knockers and message nails. They call me the gourd fairy. No cards or words go with them. Shelled-in, foolish, and hard to get started, gourds don't mean anything.

Out of the sack and in the hand,
little dry nuthin' bird-turd,
him just lay here thinkin'
I am a big fuckin' man.

You're a stupid rotten tooth.
Be like yo daddy, little
peter-in-the-wind. I spit
and thumb you in and hump

once to make you jump.
Bump up, jumpkin bumpkin,
you got this one sombitchin' chance
to be a gourd, or feed for ants.

FROM *WE'RE LAUGHING AT THE DAMAGE*
(1977)

Good night.

                  Where is he? you ask

                        in your sleep.

       Where is she I say

as we begin

    to move steadily

        against the current.

                 Good night.

      Let's give up

         on staying up.

           The right hand

        curls into the left.

                 Good night.

The top sheet

      is torn a little.   You hold one side.

     We tear it slowly

          to the edge.

    Good night.

Snow.

The hatband tight around my head.
                              and I have no hat on.

We're playing out in the snow,
              feeling no distance or time anywhere.

                    Chives, we're chives
              lying here in sour cream,
the hollow leaves of an onion.

                    That man inside there
              could cure himself
                    by looking in our faces.

                    All this water,
              slowed and almost stopped.

One line to the next,
              hold your breath no longer than that,

very calm,
              and filling quietly and quickly

like a bucket with a garden hose in it
                    under the waterlevel.

Those times, the dead

open their eyes in the ground
              thinking now I remember, yeah,

                              snow.

Putting up a bowl, its true resting
place,
inside another bowl.

This last week,

I sentence it. Take it away.

Bring in the next, and stay.

I am fixing something good:

a sweet sausage tied in a circle,

on a bed of saffron rice,

green salad with mushrooms,

red wine. Stick around.

Read me a cookbook.

A flame is walking in the dry woods,
and no harm done.

It's nine thousand mornings,
the gold light from those,

my footsteps coming toward me.

This is how we'd like
our own throats to be:

green icewater, the wet black walls,
the long pale kelp underneath,

and here a seal comes
through the arch,

he sees us, his face
a mask barely lifted.

We see his whole shape
standing in the water,

I raise one hand like a Navajo,
he hesitates,

then turns a sprinter's turn
pushing off from no wall

back through the hole,
Holes communicating with the sea,
it says on the map.

We rockclimb
up a different way than we came
and find a rainpool

locked in the cliff, mostly dried up.
Around the edge a yard in,

a fringe of bright yellow,
bright yellow slime

* * *

                                        so flowery and quick,
                              and somehow the image
                    of our silence, the way
          we can't quite talk.

Then the next day
          I go to help look
                    for Jack Harry O'Halloran.

          Three houses down,
                    He has been grieving a week
                              for his granddaughter, nineteen.
                              Jack Harry was heard up at four.
          His dog came back at dawn.

Groups of five or six,
          we are scouting the north edge.

          Nobody swims but me, islanders
                              don't swim, they point

                    to what looks like
                              Jack Harry's blue polyethylene rope
                                        In the seaweed.

                    With just tennis shoes on, against their advice

          I dive from the rock,
                    stay under longer than I need to,

                                        climb back without a word,
                    another look, another dive.

. . .

Jesus, he's like a fish,
                    ripping loose the strand
                                of dead-blue kelp to show them.

There are no fish that I have seen
                        in this inlet
                                and the seals are somewhere

            along with Jack Harry,
                        and you,

                away from this cold bright room
                                where I lengthen and magnify
                                        and almost disappear.

for my mother

Tall window
where a tree spreads
over closed eyes looking into sun,
the room in a reverie it has
when I leave: the tree, the light
a glass boat on a deep sky
full of moving ferns.

You are all around me
like a presence in a layer of dust
or a fire, or the windy
day that loosens my hold.

Quick, tell me again
how the talking song goes
about the oooold woman
waaaaay down where nooooo
body lived and noooooo
body ever came.
I can't remember.
Something about making johhnycake.

You always tickled my feet
changing the sick covers
or waking me up.
Loving the dying even,
joking with the nuns how God
told Lot to take his wife
and flee. Said he got his wife out
just in time, but he never could
find that flea.

. . .

The dogwood across the yard
the dog in the garbage
for that matter, all that's left
behind, is lying down
listening for a long barge
coming up the river. My body
has been dredged and loaded
with yours
into the moulds of that barge.

We swallowed a pin, you and I
years back in a glass of water.
There is a pin, or a needle,
or a glass of water
lost inside of us somewhere.
The image moves on the window.

Changed and changed again
the heart stays buried
in the breast. The dead
keep opening my eyes.

for my parents

To fix attention on the dead
and not let us wander off
a clamp shuts in the chest.
Lights grow faint and more numerous.
There is only the looking in.

Your palm
beneath the outer map of skin
has an old wound badly sewn up
with an ordinary white thread
healed in an ugly welt
that opens while you look.

Inside the hand, a host
the small image of a man
wrapped in membrane like a toy
that's been buried in the earth.
You've been tending him for years
within your body
loving the bare backs of women
placing your right hand in cold streams
for him, and now you know why.

What world you've known, the sky itself
is densely rooted and nerved
here in this icon
your one true pregnancy
still on the bloodvine like a melon
perfecting its stripes
with seeds and memory.

The dead are way ahead of us, thank God,
at the clean wooden tables by the waterfall

in the permanent mist
talking however they do
without using metaphor.

Left behind we meditate on something
on a pair of pliers
changing the bite, open and shut.

Wind ruffles a quilt
slowly through a week of weather.
A crowd with all ages dancing, hands in the air,
come to the presence of trees where each
inside himself rejoices
like fish or shallow rapids
or any other sign
say the edge of a door
or a man running down a flight of steps
signs the last rebirth
hasn't yet begun.

Sunday nights in the office
I pitch three times six times
and listen to the *I Ching:*

The white horse comes as if on wings

The bed is split at the edge

My overcoat
spread out in the yard
is one more text from the closet.

One every week, at least one,
reminds me, *be a nest*
be broken.
The   cemetery eats the present
We bring.

Insects build in the glass case
we come back to
morning after morning.

A dead coat speaks through my head
and has for a year.

Nights I don't dream, a face
comes close to the roof
in the overcast, a woman
with her eyes shut.

We used to unhook the hall mirror
And walk outside
holding it parallel to the ground

walking through the limbs it looked like
and out over the sky.

Let   me feel that empty again.

Let the overcoat stick
where it is
like a skindiver
facedown in the crust
learning all he can
about the stages of compost,
the intricate basketwork of snakes.

I'll get back to that,
but right now
the hall mirror of my sight
is laid out in the grass, face up
to be the middle point, the lips
of an hourglass
that has no bottom, no top,
and no sand.

Ridges flowing out of time
back to seawater.

Snakeskin from a branch above the road.
Honeycombs along the beach, black rocks
years in the water
like bits of my own erotic brain
the children find.

A stone like a smooth cinder
with three faces, one yawning.
one with a shell in its mouth,
one a skull's face.

A week without mail or telephone or news
listening to surf—
just the waking edge
falling toward sleep
repeating itself.

Waiting to the end,
for dawn.

Walking out in the tips of light
away from mirrors and windows.

Dawn: lifting
and opening a net
dripping jellies and seaweed.

Sand sinks in places
settling ahead of me on the beach.
Water moving through sand.

I.
like *goaf* that Galway Kinnell revives
in *The Book of Nightmares*
for a storage bin in a barn
or in a mine the dark place
the ore's been taken from.

A name
for my yearlong trance.
Where's Coleman.
He's back up in the goaf somewhere.

rames—skeleton, or any kind of framework,
the rames of a new house seen through the trees.
The rames of an idea. Just the rames of a man
born on a night with no moon.

Some it's hard to save.
Like *solander*, a box
made in the form of a book,
used for holding botanical specimens, papers, maps,
for hiding secret guns, shoplifting.

saprophagous

sarcophagy

So it is,
riffling the S volume of the OED
I come to *satispassion.*
It does not mean what it ought to.
Theological, for enough agony
to atone. *Deliver us not O Lord this day*
from satispassion.

2.

sauvequipeut—French for *save yourself whoever can,*
meaning a general stampede or complete rout.
Cumberland College in Sauvequipeut
at Georgia Tech, 222 to Nothing.

sawney—foolishly sentimental, whiny
with false, naïve emotion. Scottish variant
for the name Sandy.
Don't get in that sawney voice.
We won't be gone long.

Someone asked once at a reading,
Where are other people in your poems?
What if I'd said
each old word is a breathing out
of someone's name. *Sawney.*

The ear is the last face says Emily
in one of her letters.

seg—a callous of hard skin on the hand.

sejant describes a quadruped
in a sitting position with forelegs upright.

selachian—like a shark.

selenian—pertaining to the moon,
considered as a world within itself.

selcouth—self-known, known to the self,
meaning marvelous and wonderful and rare.
A constant, selcouth sound
like cicadas, or the surf.

•   •   •

St. Elmo's fire.
What am I looking for in dictionaries
but St. Elmo's fire.
The glow of atmospheric electricity
that appears as a top of light
on pointed objects
in bad weather.
Corpus sancti,
St. Elmo's breath.

Do words protect us
with their cold light?

3.
The face does look like an ear, eventually.
Words we're using now
burn out. What the point is
I don't know.

pollex—the innermost digit of the forelimb
in air-breathing vertebrates, the thumb.
Whales have thumbs.

polroz—the pit under a waterwheel.

pome as a verb, to form a compact head or heart,
as a cabbage that pomes close to the ground.

potamic—of rivers,
and things that live there, like turtles,
moons, waterwheels, cabbages,
and words that hold an image
for a moment
before they turn to sand
and silver paint.

4.
Backwards from the center
with the M volume.

musophobist—one who regards poetry
with suspicious dislike.

muskin—pretty face, sweetheart.

mimp—to purse up one's mouth, primly
in silence. She just sits there
with her muskin all mimped up.

melrose—a curative preparation
made of powdered rose leaves, honey, and alcohol.
When she looks like that,
give her some melrose.

meaze—the form that a rabbit leaves
pressed in the grass and comes home to.

maris—the womb.

Taking such small steps down the list,
alphabetically disguising
the way I say the same thing over and over:

How this is where I hide.

In a room with thirteen dictionaries
and no windows,
hide from women
who love more than I can stand
to be loved,
who want me not to hide
inside the breath of an old word,

or inside their bodies
like St. Elmo's fire
playing under the shoulder blades.

Rabelais, St. Francois,
help me out.

fanfreluche—to trifle, to act wantonly. Fanfreluching it,
thirty times a day.

grimp—to climb energetically, using hands and feet.
How the little grimper made it, I'll never know.

griggles—small apples left on the tree
by the gatherer, for the children to have.

granons—the whiskers of a cat.
Cut the granons off one side,
she'll walk in a circle.

glore—loose fat. Strange to see
two eyes waking up
in the midst of all that glore.

gillian—a flirty, feisty girl.
and right under,
gillian-a-burnt-tail, will-o-the-wisp,
a little phosphorescence in the swamp.

5.
Barnaby—the 11th of June, St. Barnabus' day, the longest
under the old calendar, hence anything long and drawn out.

battologist—someone who repeats himself a lot. From Battos,
the stammering man
who went to ask the Delphic oracle
about his voice, and all she said was,

You shall become a king in Libya.
He kept asking *What about my voice,*
Wh-What about my voice.

Now his name is the front half
to a word nobody uses.

And he one of the chief personalities
in a listpoem, of what
we no longer have in common.

6.
ferdiful—either awesome, inspiring fear,
of full of fear, or both. *Is anybody down there,*
he shouted ferdifully. *Yes,* came back
the ferdiful answer.

feriation—a cessation of work, the act of keeping
a holiday. Simple feriation was enough for the weekend.
No binges, no feasts.

fernshaw—a thicket of ferns.
Secret places among creeks
around Chattanooga
were fernshaws, and nobody knew it.

fid—a small but thick piece of anything,
as a fid of cheese, or hamburger.

fidibus—a paper match for lighting pipes.

fidicinal—of stringed instruments and those
that play them. Suddenly my fidibus
in one long fidicinal gust.

* * *

figgum—trickery. *Stop your wicked figgum,*
and play the game right.

Turning the pages with an ache,
the spine of an unopened volume
in me, leafing the pages
for I don't know what.

7.
quatch—a word, a sound. *Not one quatch*
from you two.

queachy—dense with undergrowth. The queachy woods
kept them from getting far.

quisquilious—of the nature of rubbish, or refuse.
Quisquilious Sculpture On Display In The Garden.

quodlibetical—a *quodilbet* is any question in philosophy
or theology proposed solely as an exercise in argument.
Buckley is less effective
for being so quodlibetical.

Granted, these are for collectors.
whose lives are hidden.
As mine is to me,
faced with definitions and loose ends,
moving over a big book
like a kitchen match
feeling for a rough place.

May a year ago,
the drive from midnight till four
singing and crying *too late,*
they said, the nurses.
But I talked and joked

inside the coma,
how she sat up till five a.m.
when I won Best Athlete at camp,
too excited to sleep:
What have you won
that we're staying up this late again.

Familiar moving
around the mouth and about the eyes,
and she went back.
And I held to that hand
holding her in the world, I thought,
but that's not so, or if it is,
I let go the next morning
and slept myself.

Some words we have no record of.
Some get written down
and last for centuries
before they lose their limits
and come to mean almost anything,
nonsense words.

The best is sense and nonsense both,
child and parent,
earth and sky.

Each of us has a separate face, word and name,
until we look so long at a twin,
or down at the water,
or up into nightsky
so long,
our face becomes an ear,
listening to everything.

8.
Three at random
from the supplement:

kilhag—a wooden trap to catch rabbits
and other small game. The killhags are out.
Watch your feet.

gorpen—of anything that stares in a dumb way.
The gorpen crowd at the gate.

huma—a
fabulous bird in Persian myth, so restless
that it never lights, and good fortune to anyone
it hovers directly over.

9.
Close the book
and listen.

There's a man shouting
in the middle of the street.

Get up,
for what it means.

If it's a dance,
you must dance.
If it's death,
you must die.

What a chill when it rains,
what wind.

Comes the dance
You must dance

Comes death
You can't help it

Get up.
There's a man calling
in the middle of the street.

FROM *THE JUICE* (1972)

Big Toe
running running
running   but clean
as a referee's whistle

& absolutely still
within my shoe
inside my sock:

he listens for mud

Stomach
lunch paper
sinking into

the lake surface
the lake bottom

sleeping frogs
snapping turtles

Elbow
cradling my funnybone
like a child
I did not mean to hit:

the dull ache, the surprise
at kissing myself
there

Cheek
somebody's hiding
in the drapes
I bet I know who:

No   it's just his shoes

Heart
an earthen
sound:

60 seconds later
the two all-clear
whistle notes

Brain
a flashlight
looking through the empty
limbs

Appendix
one boxing glove
laced up
and ready

Knuckles
under the bench
four helmets
look out backwards
at the cheerleaders:
each to his own

Navel
hold the phone
down here   see
if she can still
hear me gurgling:

my Long Distance
mother

Shoulder Blades
the common scallop
shell   broken in two
at its hinge

moves mystically
like it wasn't
hurt

Jaw
the first balcony:

a secret conversation
with yourself:

eating popcorn
with your ears covered

Upper Lip
the pronouns
keep changing
from *myself*
to *yourself*
and back:

during a long kiss

Adam's Apple
never said
a word:

he just nodded

Small of the Back
water shapes you
as you lean back
up against the opening
filling the pool

Crown of the Hair
with the heel
of your hand
make a round place
in the sand

Tongue
this mealy earth,
my driveway

Bags Under the Eyes
the turnaround place
at the end of a lovers' lane:

why is that car coming back

Nape
there are names
for almost everywhere
loving,

Jowl
good-natured names
like land
that's been lived on:

Cowlick, Hollow of the Back

Ear Lobe
Suck Creek, Lovers' Leap
(we all know
what happens there)

Thighs
hoist lever
in the water

constantly adjusting
their bite

Achilles Tendon
walk on your heels
across a puddle:

you mythological
beast

Wrist
minnows
are the little muscles
just under the surface

Hips
pumpkin
with pumpkin
hair and pumpkin
seeds inside

Eye
delayed light:

the flying
edge, and the wing
folded

Blood
the winery is on fire:

listen to the music

Semen
thousands
of weird little figurines
carved out of soap

suddenly come alive
and jabber like
foreigners

Cavities
the scraps of old
addresses we carry
in our wallets

Roof of the Mouth
run your tongue
all along the rafters:

moth in a Coke bottle

Middle Finger
a country boy

with one joke

always:

hey Zeke, where y'at

Genitals
the loaded question:

the slick answer

Skull
a folk remedy
for the lovesick:

share a meal
of turtle meat

then tack the shell up
for a birdhouse

Spine
a curl of rainwater
down the windshield

moves around
like it's hearing
the radio

Coccyx
fear is a rattling
in the tailbone:

my saliva
thickens

Blind Spot
what no one can see
is always a point
widening in the eye

Lymph
, in thy origins
be all my sins
remembered

Scar
the one chance
I will ever have
to go to Finland

is a long lake
frozen to my leg

Pelvis
ra great stainless
steel mixing bowl

(with me in it) floats
down the snowpath

Buttocks
oceanic pods

drifting laterally

midway down

softly thinking

(for centuries)

sunlight   sunlight

Inner Ear
the girl on the dime

gets off one night
and meets me there

Goosepimples
crowdpleasers
coming down the aisles
of my arms and legs:

crowds of the pleased
stand up and clap

Liver
a dripping locker room
full of older men

Haunches
waterwitching bones
that hunker down
on the spur of the moment
like a spell

Back of the Knee
a daily memo pad

open to the scratch
paper at the year's end

Dimple
a saltlick
for deer

Sleep
(formed in the edges)

touch the splinter

touch the white

Spleen
in man a dark purplish flattened oblong
object of a soft fragile consistency lying
near the cardiac end of the stomach
enclosed in an elastic capsule from which
bundles of fibres ramify through the tissue
of the organ which is divisible into
a loose red pulp in intimate connection
with the blood supply and a denser white
pulp chiefly of lymphoid tissue condensed
in masses about the small arteries: the
seat of emotions: the source of laughter

Fingertips
up the side
of the big dictionary

. . .

spread like waterbugs
on the open page:

my hands are close
to being words

Armpit
the nose runs a ritzy
tobacco shop where
the moment you enter

you get the idea
that your shadow
is a plume of smoke

Uvula
the always poising
little bunch
of grapes

in anybody's
orgy

Taste Buds
are soils for growing
as many varieties
of wildflower
sandwiches

Spoor
why do I keep stopping
to assign little

like
    Hangnail
or
    Spit

or
Peg Leg

the point is
this: to keep

the juice
between my

saying it and
your doing it,

you tracking
me and me you

Yawn
(   )

Tic
talk to me
talk to me

Nostrils
get the drift of things
and shape it like a key

Blush
that time
private as blood
comes to light
on my face

like a pocket pulled inside out

Halfgainer, Halftwist
let your moves

release your love

for this moment

Spit 'n Image
pouring honey
Benjamin

your face folds
out of mine

& mine is a fold
in grandaddy's sweetness
& so on

faces pour
& fold like honey

Hands
the rapids:

domes that bulge
against the current
and troughs
that sluice the whole river

Rice
inside you

my child's hand turning
in grain

in the seed
thrown over us

Caul
what is coming
twill be wrapt

in a burglar's
face for a while

until it's mine
with a new cheek

that feels just
like your leg

Shadow
cold air
between my body

and the figure
flowing down the steps

Bosoms
apples for the eye
with a tip of a tongue
in each

Balls
another double play

Birthmark
a wine stain, coffee
bourbon, who knows

what to make of it

Sound Made by Snapping the Fingers
finger releasing finger
would not seem to make
such sound, but it do

the middle one pretends to contend
with the thumb, then slides off

to hit the meaty part of the heel
of the palm, but none of those
mechanics is where the sound
comes from

the clear note arrives
from the invisible, some
inches apart from the act,
coming in on airy cellphone
lines from Polynesia, South Africa,
and Central Asia, where body
percussion is musically
honored as language

my Sri Lankan teacher, Bawa
Muhaiyaddeen, sitting on his bed,
as he always was when I knew him, once
looked at me sitting on the bedroom
floor, said, Some people grow beards
and stand in front of crowds
pretending to be wise

said, some people make their living
so easily, just by snapping
their fingers, like this,
like that, like this

* * *

they are wrong, those who say
it is harder to work with your brain
than with your hands   they are wrong

no matter   the loveliest way of going
is to do almost nothing, make only
a slight sound, be as empty as
a piece of paper with nothing on it
take a nightwalk   and then rest

for Kittsu

Floating with your head back
up to the ears in a river
you can hear a lot of lives
you didn't expect: an outboard motor
starting up beyond your sight
somebody's sinker taps against a drum
two kids are yelling mouthfuls

In the general flow
are sounds you might make yourself
and ones you can only imagine:
garfish moving along the bottom
water moccasins curling into tree roots
Chickamauga Dam upstream
imperceptibly giving way

Half in air   half in water
your eyes awake   your ears adream
with soundings   the mind can bob
and understand where it is

Alone on the shining surface
buoyed up with creatures
in such a dangerous sleep
I have created children taking chances
underwater   at night
edging with their fingers along the bluff
above the river   jumping barefooted
into a cellar full of broken glass

And one recurring child too young to know
what's risky on a ledge
curious only   about me   down here

too far away to reach him where he turns
like a dummy falling   lands flat on his back
each night   on the mattress pile of my choice

Safer in my dreams than in his
and feeling   more certain of love
that the tiny fishlike fact he was
when both of us forgot he might exist
a strange bit of marine life   sticking
there on its own   bringing up questions
of freewill and time and the possibilities
that we broke
against the motel mirror
in plain water glasses thrown to curse
and celebrate   our combining image

Wide awake   you chose   I chose   crash
following crash   not him not then   but
to lie there accepting   floating as we used to
in riverwater filled with silt   and muskrats
and sunken boats   and boys swimming

For nothing comes of choosing really
in this bed we have fallen into

Lay back your head and listen
to whatever will be with us
to the waters pressing on each eardrum
for the life inside

rocking motion of remembering   red pig-iron gate latch
now my feet are on the tree roots   just inside the fence
hyaah hayaaah to scare him away   like I've seen done
this goat with eyes broken red inside   his head even
with mine   the horns glance off my shoulder into ivy
the screen door that I run to   is locked from inside
a hoof on the step behind me   then his goatface dressed
in a strand of ivy   waiting for me to take hold of
years ridged into horn   conch shell in my hands
slowly rocking side to side   neither of us with arms
deadlocked in a zodiac of child & goat   a period piece
without a sound or a cry   but moving on its own

The evergreen seasonal ridge of the past
                    has no real name.

Stringer's

       is two hills over
and famous

       but this other
              with so many sides and differences
is not
       so we used the wrong name

One way down was the west
       but I never have tried that.
          They were scared
       when I slipped toward the edge
             on the loose stones
                  and they should have been.

      pine cliffs
with railroad track at the bottom
            and a long view across half
the Tennessee and Williams Island and the other half
        waist high into Elder Mountain

They were too young for that look
       anyhow
           so I started back another way

      cut into the west end
is a cove gulley full of vines

  . . .

one bankside's shining mudface
                    free of leaves
waits for the backswing
              if you didn't jump
                        at the very last thinking

                  something

I was that pendulum of earth-time
                    climbing up the ridge
          into the late air

      high above the corn rows and the diesel going home

            on the steep west bluff
earth-knowing for a year
              before I set out leading children myself thirteen

singlefile
      up the easy middle path
            that was lined off for a horse trail
                  with little logs
                        and cleaned-up branches

        the east is a holy room
            owls standing on the wet limbs
      with no leaves anywhere
                      just a thin roof
                  of pine boughs
        and trailing vines on the floor:

        black trunks stand around like elders
        and keep you from scaring the owls

      a footfall   in the odd light.

  . . .

The fourth way
      slips between

      the Christmas trees
    along red washed-out places
          on the south side
      where briars grow
   that no one can run through
    no matter how scared

and a last way down
         off behind
     some locked greenhouses
         I can never sneak into now:

       too old to be curious
      about how it is to go
    a different way,
but here I am
     still trying not to find a way down
Stringer's Ridge
     with all my children though they begin to whine

      trying some way to take all the paths
and then not be down

      to love in all directions
and show the secret places to five more
              bands of children:
the bush horns and the cars are signaling
          like hawks and crows:
we can hear them through the leaves

         warning us

. . .

to pick one way
            and be down
off Stringer's Ridge.

            Link hands little no-names
with your scruffy leader.

      This hill is a vague green trance
            that I prolong.

Walk out and away
            from the ivy house.
                  Mark the place of no return

            here,

            say we are late but not ashamed.

      Bunched together down there
                  like a posse
            you can tell they are worried

                  but now they see us
            walking out
                  through the ivy
                  we are all crying
                        why are we crying

                  afraid we wouldn't get down   afraid
                        we won't go back

hurt

            that we seem to be lost.

A snake was dancing in the waterfall.
I don't know what kind.
We were about halfway up Middle Creek
as it comes down Signal Mountain
our first summer out of college
jumping from big rock
to little precarious rock
when we saw this snake dancing
like a Hindu's rope
in a little offhand waterfall.
Nevermind what allusions
occur to me now.
All of them occurred to us then
that summer of many animals
and all of them put to rout
with our thumping:
the motorboat left running by itself
in a circle   mumbling at the two of us
coupled in the water
on a submerged stump
at three in the afternoon
with aunts and uncles
coming in the front door back too early
calling Is Anybody Home
while we slip into the Chevrolet
naked as rabbits and always getting away
but never really to ourselves
unless it was laughing at that literal snake
dancing in his waterfall.

To make a yard
and then think about it
I filled in
between the retaining wall
and the steps
saving what little
dirt for last

The old sofa
went first   then
boxes of psychology
textbooks   a drop-leaf
table with two legs off
(which reminds me)
a pile of mulching
dead limbs and cuttings
flowers   a checkerboard
sacks of garbage periodically

There was a bony radiator
we threw in
for sacrificial goat
and a refrigerator
hands tied behind him
stood on the edge
oblivious   frozen with dignity
I inspected him for valuables
shut the door gently
like buttoning the top button
on a monument
and pushed him over backwards
on the passionate heap
like my best friend

• • •

The yard held its breath
shut in that icebox
for five years
before a boysize graveplot
sunk in freshly on it

Someone might have seen it happen
watery hands picking at the hinges
then after so long
as for a birthday   the breath
released   a soul spreads
into the ground   saying

take it easy   take it easy

The afterlife is not
such a problem

Deposit your old bones
and wornout appliances
so they won't explode
in a   cave-in that
might horrify someone
who doesn't know he's
aalready under the grass
all flesh is

Getting fat and tired and thirty
don't despair at being
something older   something else
What you are is lovely
Andrew Wyeth decay
a shed full of implements
beginning to become land again
part of somebody's yard

. . .

The field numbing with yesterday's rain
bloating with liquor and drying out
for the thousandth time
and you   in the midst of it
sighing once for your age
are the slow seeping back and forth
of man into earth
of earth into air

Do not ask of me
I am the hooded one

We are here to consult the entrails
for your departure.
About my cave are several signs of life
on the verge of their future
which may be read collectively or not
according to your mood.
Notice that I have no scroll or prepared text
as we approach the first enigma.

This squashed pigeon says one thing.

> *You are still young*

And this black mule, still bubbling,

> *Do not submit yourself*
> *to your own mind*

Upon the cistern ledge this fish
inside a fish inside a fish records that

> *Life is passed*
> *in the simplest of circles*
> *not in the expanding universe*
> *where everyone's mythologies overlap*

And the wormy goat stomach,
what do you think it means? Look closer.
What do you think?
It is an admission that

. . .

All advice is vague
and plagiarized

Ah look, they fly, they fly away,
my beautiful birds, my gulls . . .
an omen of another sort which means,

> *A number of changes will come*
> *and leave you depressed*

The fire there which, as you see, is going out,
will go out, and this garbage will begin to rot
tomorrow, which means something else again,

> *We shall be left with fragments*
> *of an order that is not our own*

And as you pack these secrets up
and leave me here among   my vitals
with a lot of emptied animals,
I must insist that you mean well.

Your recollection burns in my lantern,
shadows me down this ancient ear.
My eyes relax in darkness for your sight.

My hands touch stone that wears water
and I am almost out of sight now almost
gone, but listen for me. I mean to be lost

for years surviving to come out somewhere
telling a tomfool story to filling stations
and chenille shops that will have heard it

before: beneath this place your version,
you long drink of water, is yodeling
like a bloodstream, garbled sleeping sound.

You are here beside me wondering
If I know where I'm going. You are
there inside singing to a swarming

room. You are the survivor who
found another way out. The cave
itself is nothing but your skull.

You take me past the ribs and keelson
of a pleasure boat through the broken
teeth of an admission stile to where

the audience doesn't remember you
with bear hugs for a stranger—to
blank holes filled with history:

• • •

the Nickajack tribe and the Union troops
and myself fallen shattered from the ceiling
You stand with me like sleeping rubble

dreaming of form, and you nap in these
cubbyholes hanging upsidedown
folded in a brotherhood of yourself.

⸻

This cave confuses us. Meld of rock
and dung and water. Our voices blend
in a noise that tumbles the lock

of the hill and lets us out—in a chord
that starts the sacred harp again
humming in the earth like a dynamo:

What wondrous love is this
O my soul   O my soul

Postal Area #29, Los Angeles

Twice recently, young girls
              have given me the finger.
The first was on the freeway,

she sitting close to her boyfriend
              turned with sure purpose and aimed
at prominence, seatbelted in

two lanes over. The chemical shock to
              my system made me feel so like
they wanted I chased them

for miles trying to think of something
              to yell back. The second a few
minutes ago, standing beside

a drugstore, would have been easy to go
              back by, but I just waved like
oh another one. It must be

something in the atmosphere, Scorpio
              on the ascendant, or maybe they
were bored with the just looking

and better this than what I didn't give,
              much better. With one buzzoff
finger she became the mother

of my invention with her red shirt
              and her hip-huggers
              and her flowered vinyl belt:

Hey cat lady, you eat it.

get up under a mule
sometime and look   you

may have heard wrong
the equipment's all there

dormant   dreaming
of some great mythical

union between species
like Leda & her swan

or the god-bull & Europa
the mule is an aristocrat, one

of the last classical allusions
in this illiterate world

more sensual than any
theologian's dream: the double
penis ornamented with fringe,
spikes, and sexy designs
like a Deluxe from the Devil's
condom machine: all ripple
and blind wiggling lust
he can keep one going
and one resting for a full
twenty-four hours and she
can hatch his children
for two years afterward:
man makes his myths
and the snake believes them

in the big dictionary
my hand always feels
how slick and neat
the page of imperial
flags, the old ones
little ensign flags
within flags for crown
colonies, moon & stars
& dhows for the Near East
flamboyant clusters
of drums & guidons
for the smallest islands
Tobago   Caledonia
the strong indigenous beasts
of Siam   Malaya
against a white field
or green   such treasure
for some boy's collection
each to be cut out and labeled
in the ledger he tucks away
with gusty, secret plans.
But I was looking up a word

cark

The Moores left us their dog
to take care of, our namesake
Barks, but on a whim
I started calling him Carks.
Such a terror he is
scattering warfare at the poor
hedge rabbits like a phantom squad
that never needs to reload
and catching nothing but ticks.

The porch ashtray is full
of the seared little drunkards.
No one gets any good sleep
or work done with that
hangdog   underdog around.
What to do with Barks
look at this

1 cark /kark/vb (ME *carken,* lit.to to load, burden,
fr. ONF *carquier,* fr. LL *carricare*) vt: WORRY
vt: to be anxious
2 cark n: TROUBLE, DISTRESS

But that did not take care of Barks.
He was still there
in spite of how I could fancy his name up
and pencil it to the flag page.

When the sun began to go down
nothing could lure him into arm range
or even rock range.
So one day in the middle of the day
when he was tired
and sacked out in his bones
from a nightful of alarms,
I loaded him in the backseat
and took him to the SPCA.
I'd like to give you a dog.
    What's the matter?
He barks all night.
    It will cost you $5.
It's worth it.
    What's his name?
Barks.
    Fits.
Yes. Thank you very much.

Not at all.
Come back to see us,
Mr.
But I was out the door
before he could learn
my crazy name.

Headfirst in the kneehole
stretched out with my back
on the cool linoleum floor:

The underside of my swivel
chair is a printing press.
This bulletin is just out:

NOTICE
To Duplicate this Desk or if
any Repairs or Keys are or-
dered state Information Below.

JASPER OFFICE FURNITURE CO.
Jasper, Indiana

Desk (Table) No . . . .
Finish . . . .
Cabinet Maker . . . .
Date Made . . . .
Inspected By . . . .
Finish Sanded By . . . .
Rubbed By . . . .
Trimmed By . . . .
Drawer Lock Key No . . . .
Drawer Pull No . . . .
Inspected By . . . .

(Fill in the empty graffiti
blanks yourself)

Why two Inspected Bys?
That last must be the Inspector-General.

. . .

I would like to meet the man
who makes these places for us.

Places not absolutely private
(Someone could look in the window
and see my legs and feet) or
soundproof (there is a sympathetic
humming with the air conditioning) but

suitable for the professional nap.
They   might be marketed as indoor

gazebos (quartersize) or special
new supine confessionals (with
drawers) or thinking cells (fully
paneled): a shepherd's hut

Hiking in the Alps at dusk I come upon this shelter
dry and clean   I have been here a week now
deliriously happy   When I decide to leave I will
climb the next ridge and see the towers of a town
I had no idea was so close to civilization

   The desk drawer pushes out
   from the back. A beautiful blank
   space reveals itself. I ought to
   write something there: Mickey
   loves Virginia May 29, 1842—
   5th Illinois cavalry—Croatian

The mailcoach: stowed away in the compartment where
freshly cut flowers are shipped. On either side of me
long-stemmed roses and six-foot irises are trying to stay
alive by lying very still   I am a gift for somebody

   who knocks on the office door.
   Two little questioning raps.

I will never know who it was.
No footsteps coming or going.
My big clomping shoes are floating
three feet above the bookshelf.

Sent to repair the split face of a giant wooden man,
St. Jude, who stares out over Helsinki   He has a clockface
in his forehead   two hundred feet from the ground   I am
clinging dangerously to the inside of one of his coffin-
shaped nostrils   How could they expect me to use hammer
and nail up here when all my strength must be saved for
hanging on   It occurs to me now that this is the only way
to fix a saint's face, the crack in his features slowly
healing for the pendulum of my weight in his sinuses
I am the famous Helsinki Boogerman, special counsel
to the wooden clergy   Hello up in there,
ole silent father, Hello behind the clock

God of the Cave this afternoon
I am dormant finally in a ceremony
sleep is a part of.

beneath whatever kind of shirt
his shoulders are whales again
moving now under gardens in Italy

his face turns like a monastery
in the afternoon

his feet begin to loosen
and make furrows in the soil

his elbows rise
from gravel to perch

the trees fill up their lungs
and wait

when he arrives
we stand up and stretch ourselves
like the fingers of his hand

It is so easy to say
I want a new life
in the form of some new shoes
a new darkblue turtleneck
and a big scruffy poncho
for poetry reading
a whole new set of people
a new wife new town
new children. So have one.

Stretch like the cat in her sleep.

A tissue catches fire
in a child's hand
and floats up burning
out of a basement window.

I am hunched over, standing
inside a waterfall,
and I can spot figures out there.
Watery bodies
come clear to one eye,
clear and then gone

and I am just as much of a blur,
a nameless hump in the shower,
hoping, with this poem,
to go with it down
that slick place
into the drink
of a swim, my shoulders
in the moving body.

Scrapwood Man
Wine Poems—The book I was reading was *Selected Poems, Po Chu-i,* tr.
Burton Watson, Columbia University Press (New York, 2000), pp. 66, 68,
65, and others.

from There Ain't Nothing Like It—This is an expandable poem consisting of
overheard conversations, some of which I participated in and others not.

Losing It—The Emily Dickinson poem reads as follows in the original:

#520

God made a little gentian—
It tried— to be a Rose—
And failed—and all the Summer laughed—
But just before the snows

There rose a Purple Creature—
That ravished all the Hill—
And Summer hid her forehead—
And Mockery—was still—

The Frosts were her condition—
The Tyrian would not come
Until the North—invoke it—
Creator—Shall I—bloom?

Just This Once—This Bush letter/poem was first spoken on March 15, 2003
in the National Cathedral in Washington a few days before the American
invasion of Iraq began.

Tentmaking

Tentmaking—The metaphor of our collective soulmaking being the many, seemingly in conflict, crafts of constructing a tent is found in Rumi's Discourse #1. See A. J. Arberry's translation, *Discourses of Rumi*, Samuel Weiser (New York, 1960), p. 58.

Divination—In seven centuries of male lyric poetry in English I have not found that the phrase "my erect penis" has ever occurred. Galway Kinnell writes beautifully phallic passages but without using that phrase. It probably occurs somewhere, but if it does not, the glaring omission now stands rectified. *Smoor* is an Irish word for the wet haze over a bog. *Aye, just the smoor of love crossed her eyes.*

Question—Candlemas is February 2nd.

Bill Matthews Coming Along—Bill died suddenly in November 1997. I have heard he was getting ready to go out to the opera. His great and generous, elegant, tender, raffish laughter is there in the poems. It will help keep us sane. See *Selected Poems and Translations* (1969–1991), Houghton Mifflin.

Bridge—*O slow of heart.* The resurrected Jesus says this to his disciples in Emmaus, Luke 24:25.

Luke and the Duct Tape—Add Drugs carries duct tape now, under the post office counter, so it may be that poetry can make something happen. I know the store owners read this poem. And I have learned that Luke was married, and had been for eight years. His wife Tiffany tells me they were planning to have children. The last name is pronounced *poo-shay.*

The Ant—In Daniel 3:25 Shadrack, Meshach, and Abednego are bound and cast into the fiery furnace by King Nebuchadnezzar because they refuse to bow to idols. One of the king's councilors reports, *Lo I see four men loose, walking in the midst of the fire, and they have no hurt; and the form of the fourth is like the Son of God.* (King James)

Abscission Leaf, Looking into Water—I am interested in exactly where the abscission leaf is located on any particular gingko tree, if such a leaf exists. As far as I can determine, the mystery of why gingko tree leaves fall all at once, or on the same day, remains as enigmatic as how a flock of flying birds turn, suddenly all together, in a single morphogenetic field.

1971 and 1942—*O who could have foretold / that the heart grows old?* is the refrain from "A Song," *The Collected Poems of W. B. Yeats*, ed. Richard Finneran, Scribner, rev. 2nd ed., 1989, p. 139. The one who has made himself a saint of lust is my friend, Tom Mac Intyre, the Irish poet and playwright.

Lard Gourd—John Seawright did research in Georgia newspapers of the nineteenth century. Almost every day he read them on microfilm and took extensive notes. He found this dog story. I do not know the reference. He also told me of a filler note he found. It was observed that sailors back from the slave trade route (West Africa, the Caribbean, New England, England, then back to West Africa) in the ports of Bristol and Cardiff had begun saying *So long* to each other, in imitation of the Muslim slaves Salaam aleichem. Now we casually, especially in the South, wish each other the Islamic *Peace of God*, mixing sacred traditions. I hope it is true.

Driving Back from the Mountains—I did not remember it while writing this, but Whitman has a poem called "So Long!" in which he says goodbye to poetry. "My songs cease, I abandon them . . . I feel like one who has done work for the day to retire awhile . . . I love you. I depart from materials. I am as one disembodied, triumphant, dead."

Elegy for John Seawright—The poet, writer, historian, polymath, artist, cook, and friend, John Seawright, died at age forty-four on May 9, 2001, of a brain aneurysm.

In "The Marriage of Heaven and Hell" William Blake says that if the doors of perception are cleansed, everything will appear infinite and holy. This will come to pass by "an improvement of sensual enjoyment," p. 154, Keynes' Blake. (All Blake references are to *Blake: Complete Writings*, ed. Geoffrey Keynes, Oxford University Press, 1959.) The Henry Vaughan poem quoted is "The World."

"But not today." In response to someone's calling out from a conference audience Blake's Proverb of Hell, "The road to excess leads to the palace of wisdom" (p. 150), Robert Bly turned his head away and shot back, "But not today."

"Drive your cart and your plow over the bones of the dead," another Proverb of Hell (p. 150), balances with my tendency to visit the tombs of dead Sufis and listen for their zikr of remembering.

"The cry of the parrot . . ." Blake does not mention parrots or turtles. He says, "The tygers of wrath are wiser than the horses of instruction" (p. 152). A parrot will sometimes repeat what he is told inside a cage, whereas turtles, those free-wandering pilgrims, mostly keep quiet.

"Exuberance is beauty" is another of Blake's proverbs (p. 152).

"Inlets of soul." Blake's Devil says, "Man has no Body distinct from Soul, for that called Body is a portion of Soul discerned by the five senses, the chief inlets of Soul in this age" (p. 149).

The crows walking in sand at the end of this poem—I hear John, *Well, you got those crows in there; can't have a self-respecting elegy with crows.* John was a fabulous walker around Athens. Everybody remembers his long-legged lope. He was always looking for something, and he always found it. Beauty you might call it, if you were Plotinus.

Another Seawright story. In August 1967 I arrive in Georgia from southern California to take an assistant professorship in the English Department at the University of Georgia. It is Sunday night. I am alone in Barnett's Newsstand in downtown Athens. For some reason I have no money with me. On the turnaround stand I see a 75-cent Mentor paperback, *The Essential Plotinus.* I have always been drawn to Plotinus. I wrote a term paper in graduate school on neoplatonism in Spenser's "Mutabilitie Cantos." On that Sunday night, though, I own no Plotinus, and I badly want to go home and read him. My spiritual longing is such that I steal the book. I do not remember how I got it out the door, what I did to hide the crime, but I did take it. I still have it.

I told this incident to John Seawright. He got very quiet and looked like he could not believe what I was saying. It turns out that John Seawright stole the same book from the library of the honors dorm when he was a student there in the early 1970s. Lipscomb Hall. It is the only book that either of us ever stole. *The Essential Plotinus,* translated with commentary by Elmer O'Brien. Father Elmer, S.J., a Jesuit. You can believe this or not. I do not care. I know that it happened. And of course, as I am inclined to do, I hear such synchronicities as a kind of conversation with the universe. Look here, a couple of book thief friends. What is translation, say the French, but thievery and betrayal?

I was reading recently in my stolen Plotinus, p. 131, the image of daylight entering the houses of a town, "spreading itself among the houses without being split up, all the while remaining whole." I felt the delight of knowing that Jelaluddin Rumi had looked at these very words. "Sunlight looks slightly different on this wall than it does on that wall, and a lot different on this other one, but it is all one light" (p. 48, *The Soul of Rumi*). It becomes the central metaphor for how Rumi dissolves the barriers between religions. The impulse to praise, like the variations of sunlight, is all one thing. Differences are not important.

I recounted this mystical rip-off to my friend Judy Long as we were walking the streets of Athens. We went in to Barnett's to verify the poet Stephen Dunn's claim that he had been reviewed in *Oprah*. He had. We read the short review standing in the store. We did not by the *Oprah*, I don't think. We bought something, and at the cash register I said, "I stole a 75 cent book in here in 1967, and I would like to give you this $10." I handed the bill to the slightly amused man, who held it without seeming to know where he should put it.

John Seawright's Epitaph—Slightly altered from Seamus Heaney's "The Walk," in *The Spirit Level*, Farrar, Straus, and Giroux, 1996, p. 74. Many people thought that when John died, it was of a broken heart. His beautiful wife Cynthia had passed away in an automobile accident in December 1993.

Club: Granddaughter Poems
No Finale—Briny is a nickname for Bryan, my granddaughter. Elizabeth Vincent Bryan was my mother's maiden name.

The Juice
Sound Made by Snapping the Fingers—The Body Poem sequence was written in the spring of 1968. This final, more garrulous poem, was added in the winter of 2006.